SECOND EDITION

THE
CIVIL RIGHTS
MOVEMENT
IN
AMERICA

from 1865 to the Present

By Patricia and Fredrick McKissack

Consultants: Jim Haskins, Professor of English,
University of Florida, Gainesville, Florida and
Harry S. Ashmore, author of *Hearts and Minds* and
Epitaph For Dixie

CHILDRENS PRESS®
CHICAGO

Editorial Staff

1st ed. project editor: Mary Reidy
2nd ed. project editor: E. Russell Primm III
Editor: Charnan Simon
Cover design: Biner Design
Interior design: Karen Yops
Photo research: Alice Flanagan, Judith Feldman
Indexer: Kathryn Cairns
Proofreader: Irene Keller

Photo acknowledgments appear on pages 350 and 351

Library of Congress Cataloging-in-Publication Data

McKissack, Pat, 1944–
     The Civil Rights Movement in America from 1865 to the
present/by Patricia and Fredrick McKissack. — 2nd ed.
p. cm.
     Includes bibliographical references and index.
     Summary: From the beginning of Reconstruction to the
present, traces the struggle of blacks to gain their civil rights
in America, with a brief comparison of their problems to those
of other minorities.
     ISBN 0-516-00579-0
     1. Afro-Americans—Civil rights—Juvenile literature.   2. Afro-
Americans—History—Juvenile literature.   3. United
States—Race relations—Juvenile literature.   4. Civil rights
movements—United States—History—Juvenile literature.
[1. Afro-Americans—Civil rights.   2. Afro-Americans—
History.   3. United States—Race relations.]
I. McKissack, Fredrick. II. Title.
E185.61.M479 1991
973'.0496073—dc20
                                                          91-4103
                                                               CIP
                                                                AC

Contents

Foreword

Pat and Fred McKissack have written a marvelous history of the Civil Rights Movement for junior high and high school readers. Young adults naturally have no direct experience of what conditions were like for black Americans a mere twenty-five years ago—after all, they were not even born—but if they are to understand their world, and make their own place in it, then they must have an understanding of what has gone before and how past events affect the present.

There have been many histories of the Civil Rights Movement. The failing of the great majority of them is that they separate the years of the 1950s and 1960s—the marches and sit-ins and freedom rides, and the civil rights and voting rights laws that such activities were designed to bring about—from what occurred in the years before and after those two decades. The McKissacks have treated civil rights from a broader historical perspective, tracing the movement from the era of slavery to the present, and thus making the events of the 1950s and 1960s much easier to understand.

Most other civil rights histories also feature only the major players in the civil rights drama. The McKissacks manage to include many of the less well-known people who made important and lasting contributions. They also include a large number of women who, with the exception of Rosa Parks, are often neglected in comparable histories.

The great advantage of the McKissacks' book is that it is so interestingly written and so enjoyably readable that it can be read as a straight narrative from cover to cover. At the same time, it can be used as a valuable reference tool by those who want a brief biography of a civil rights personality or a short explanation of a particular event. It is the most factual and up-to-date volume that I know to exist, and it should be in every junior high and high school library.

Jim Haskins
Professor of English
University of Florida
Gainesville, Florida
Fall 1986

Introduction

This is an introductory book about the American civil rights movement from 1865 to the present. We condensed the more than 120-year struggle for freedom and justice into three parts, and highlighted key people, places, and events that were involved.

Although civil rights are commonly associated with black Americans, other groups have had to overcome social injustices, religious intolerance, racial discrimination, and degrading segregation. Therefore, we included parts of their stories as well—Native Americans, Asians, Hispanics, women, immigrants, handicapped, and children.

Man's quest for justice didn't begin in twentieth-century United States. Actually, the story of "rights" had no beginning or end. From ancient times to the present, the struggle for rights has been at the core of countless social and political conflicts. But even though the concepts of rights are constantly being reevaluated, *life and freedom* are the universally accepted basis for *human rights*. Human rights are the foundation upon which our entire democracy is based.

Civil rights are the social and political privileges guaranteed to all citizens regardless of race, sex, religion, or national origin. But freedom, justice, and equality are just high-sounding words unless protective laws are impartially enforced. In America the United States Constitution is the legal document designed to provide and protect an individual's rights and also those of groups and organizations.

The Founding Fathers of the American republic knew that slavery was a mockery of human rights. There was no way the two systems could coexist. We began our book at that point in history when slavery was abolished, and the Thirteenth, Fourteenth, and Fifteenth Amendments were passed, giving the freedmen all the privileges of citizenship. The story might have been different from this point on. But a few people interpreted the Constitution for their own dead-end purposes, and America became a segregated nation. It took another hundred years of long and bitter struggle before the rights spelled out in the earlier constitutional amendments would be realized by all U.S. citizens. And, still the struggle continues.

Throughout the preparation of the book we made tough decisions about what to include and what to exclude, but never without careful consideration. For example, a very successful bus boycott was held in Baton Rouge, Louisiana in 1953. We chose to feature the Montgomery boycott of 1957, because it is historically targeted as the beginning of the "Modern Civil Rights Movement." Also it was in Montgomery that Dr. Martin Luther King, Jr., established himself as a nonviolent protest leader.

We hope this book will help answer some of your questions, introduce names and events in an easy-to-understand chronology, and, finally, generate interest that will lead you to more detailed accounts of the civil rights movement in America.

Fredrick and Patricia McKissack
St. Louis, Missouri

Introduction to the Second Edition

This second edition reflects the course that the struggle for civil rights has taken since the first edition was published in 1987.

The updated material clearly shows how frustratingly slow the civil rights movement has become. After all the years of political and social action, the constitutional guarantees of equality and justice remain an unfulfilled promise for many Americans.

As we approach the twenty-first century, women and minorities are still battling underemployment, staggering poverty, poor medical care, inferior education, and substandard housing. Who can pick up a magazine or newspaper without reading about the controversial debates regarding affirmative action, women's rights, gay and lesbian rights, rights for the disabled, even the rights of the unborn? These and many other issues remain unresolved, but they are not being ignored. The struggle continues. And that's a healthy sign.

We want this second edition of *The Civil Rights Movement in America from 1865 to Present*, with more current information about people, places, and events, to inform and inspire you to become more involved. People who worked with other people helped change America. It will take that same spirit to keep America moving forward. To paraphrase a folk saying:

We aren't what we ought to be;

We aren't what we want to be;

We aren't what we're gonna be;

But thank Providence,

We aren't what we were!

Fredrick and Patricia McKissack
May 1991

Part I

One Step Forward; Two Steps Back

THE U.S. TROOPS REMOVED.
NO MORE FEDERAL INTERFERENCE
AND BAYONET RULE.
THE CARPET—BAGGERS GONE.
NO MORE RADICAL RULE, AND
FAMILY FEUDS.
THE NIGGERS ARE
GOING. — THEN WE
WILL HAVE NO MORE
NIGGER INSURRECTIONS
OR WAR OF RACES.

A former slave tells his former master that he is going North.

TIME LINE 1865-1875

1865   Lee surrenders to Grant—Civil War ends; Freedmen's Bureau established; Abraham Lincoln assassinated; Thirteenth Amendment ratified; southern states pass the black codes

1866   Passage of the Civil Rights Act; Ku Klux Klan organized in Pulaski, Tennessee; Fourteenth Amendment passed by Congress

1867   Reconstruction Act

1868   President Andrew Johnson's impeachment trial; President Ulysses S. Grant elected

1869   Fifteenth Amendment passed by Congress

1870   Civil Rights Act of 1870; Enforcement Act of 1870-1871; Peacekeeping troops sent to the South

1872   Amnesty Bill passed by Congress

1875   Civil Rights Act of 1875

A photo taken on April 2, 1865, shows the devastation of Richmond, Virginia.

_1865-1875_

RECONSTRUCTION BEGINS

General William T. Sherman and sixty thousand Union soldiers were marching from Atlanta to the sea, cutting a three-hundred-mile path of destruction. The South lay in ruins. It was senseless to go on fighting. At Appomattox Court House on April 9, 1865, Robert E. Lee, commander of the Confederate army, surrendered to Ulysses S. Grant, general of the Union army. The Civil War was over. It was time to rebuild.

For southern blacks the end of the war meant the end of slavery. Four million former slaves were experiencing "freedom" for the first time. Although most of the freedmen had no education, no money, no employment, and, in many cases, no place to live, they cherished the idea of freedom and the hope that it offered future generations of black Americans. Hope that—with freedom, education, and guaranteed rights—jobs and a better way of life would come. It was with this hope that they began to rebuild. What a time for rejoicing!

For southern whites the end of the war meant the fall of "King Cotton" and their old way of life, a life-style that had been supported by slavery. The large plantations that had been the

People in Washington, D.C. celebrate the abolishment of slavery.

hallmark of southern economic pride lay wasted in defeat. Proud Southerners, even those who were too poor to have owned slaves, refused to accept freedmen as citizens who had rights equal to their own. Some die-hards migrated to South and Central America with their slaves. The majority, who remained, began rebuilding with fierce determination, but bitterly opposing any changes.

Immediately following the Civil War, responsible leaders recognized that the freedmen would need help adjusting. Between 1865 and 1875 the United States government passed laws that helped provide and protect the rights of all free people in the United States. This period was called Reconstruction because the result was supposed to be a reconstructed society that included people of all races. However, except for the brief Reconstruction period, blacks and other minorities never really experienced freedom and justice as guaranteed to them by the Constitution.

Before the Emancipation Proclamation, slave owners enjoyed cheap labor. After the slaves were freed, social and economic conditions changed for both the whites and blacks.

Southern leaders argued that the government was misusing its authority by granting former slaves equal rights and protection under the law. "White supremacy" became the rallying cry around which these people gathered. And "states' rights" became the political means used to pass and uphold unjust laws. The failure of Reconstruction and the subsequent passage of segregation laws in the late 1800s can be traced directly to the struggle between states' rights and the authority of the central government.

STATES' RIGHTS VERSUS THE CENTRAL GOVERNMENT

The United States government is a federal system that divides power between the national and the state governments. The national government has the power, among other things, to enforce constitutional laws. Each state has the authority to regulate matters within its borders as long as they are within constitutional law. That was the problem. Laws and the interpretation of the laws were seen differently by those who advocated states' rights and those who wanted a strong central government. During Reconstruction the conflict reached another crisis.

When Andrew Jackson was president, there had been a serious confrontation between those who favored the rights of states and those who believed in the authority of the central government. States' righters, led by John C. Calhoun, believed that a state could, or should, refuse to obey an oppressive federal law. This action led to the nullification crisis of 1832. President Jackson responded by asking for, and receiving from Congress, the power to use military means to enforce federal laws.

After the Civil War, southern states again challenged the

government's power. States' righters, who at the time were mostly Southerners, protested that the government was overstepping its bounds by interceding on behalf of former slaves in the areas of education, employment, voting rights, and other "state controlled" matters. The national government counterargued that the constitutional rights of the former slaves were being denied and that it was therefore the responsibility of the federal government to be involved. National leaders made it clear that they would carry out their duties to all citizens without interference from the states or they would use force if necessary.

President Abraham Lincoln pushed for strong national legislation regarding the freedmen. To safeguard the rights of the four million former slaves, Congress passed, and the states ratified, the Thirteenth, Fourteenth, and Fifteenth Amendments. The Freedmen's Bureau was also established to help make the transition from bondage to freedom easier. But the southern states answered the national government with state laws called the "black codes."

A government-sponsored freedmen's village in Arlington, Virginia

LINCOLN AND THE FREEDMEN

The Back-to-Africa Plan

At the end of the Civil War, there were four million former slaves. Some left the South, but an overwhelming majority remained. For a time there was a question about how to handle these newly freed people. President Abraham Lincoln, the man who had emancipated the slaves, briefly considered a plan that included sending blacks to Haiti, South America, or Liberia in Africa. As retold in Carl Sandburg's *Abraham Lincoln: The War Years*, President Lincoln told a delegation of black men, "Your race are suffering, in my judgment, the greatest wrong inflicted on any people. But even when you cease to be slaves, you are yet far removed from being placed on an equality with the white. . ."

This was not a new idea. As early as 1817 Robert Finley had founded the American Colonization Society to return freed black

Over three hundred blacks emigrated to Liberia from Savannah, Georgia, on March 1, 1896, on the steamship Laurada.

slaves to Africa. In 1822 the society had begun transporting former slaves to Liberia, a country on Africa's western coast. By 1847 eleven thousand blacks had resettled in Monrovia, which became the capital of the independent Republic of Liberia. After the Civil War the back-to-Africa movement appealed to some blacks who chose to return to Africa. There are also records showing that, at the government's expense, four hundred freedmen voluntarily went to Haiti, an island in the Caribbean Sea. Within a year, the colony was wiped out by a smallpox epidemic.

The majority of people—black and white—rejected the back-to-Africa solution to the race issue. In an open letter to President Lincoln, a group of black leaders responded to this plan:

> Mr. President . . . This is our country by birth, consequently we are acclimated and in other respects better adapted to it than to any other country. This is our native country; we have as strong attachment naturally to our native hills, valleys, plains, luxuriant forests, flowing streams, mighty rivers, and lofty mountains as any other people.

A group of clergymen also argued that it was immoral to enslave a people, to force them to help build a nation, and then to dump them when they were no longer needed.

Other opponents to the plan pointed out that black Americans were neither African nor European but rather the offspring of both. Through the intermixing of the races on the plantations, a new race had developed that was uniquely American. "Nor can we fail to feel a strong attachment to the whites with whom our blood has been commingling from the earliest days of this our country. Neither can we forget and disown our white kindred. This is the country of our choice, being our fathers' country."

Before long it became clear to all involved that blacks had helped found, build, and defend the United States. They had been on this continent since 1619. They were as much a part of this country as was any other group that claimed citizenship. Would an American whose father had landed at Plymouth consider going back to England? This was unthinkable. The freedmen made it clear that they too were in America to stay. It seemed advisable to adopt some other plan, one that would safeguard the rights of all citizens. And Lincoln followed that advice.

The Thirteenth Amendment

President Lincoln had two goals: to rebuild the South and to aid the former slaves in beginning their lives as free people. To that end, under pressure from the president and others, Congress proposed the Thirteenth Amendment to the Constitution, which outlawed slavery in America. President Lincoln signed the Thirteenth Amendment on February 1, 1865, and it was ratified on December 18, 1865. It simply stated that

> Neither slavery nor involuntary servitude, except as a punishment for crime whereof the party shall have been duly convicted, shall exist within the United States or any place subject to their jurisdiction.
>
> Congress shall have power to enforce this article by appropriate legislation.

At the time, the amendment protected blacks from being reenslaved in the South. But the law goes far beyond that moment in history. The Thirteenth Amendment ended slavery forever in the United States and protected *any* group of people from being enslaved in this country.

The Freedmen's Bureau

Men of good reason knew that, without education and employment, no group could achieve economic equality. So in early 1865 Congress passed an act to establish the Freedmen's Bureau, which would be in force for one year. The purpose of the Freedmen's Bureau was twofold: (1) to provide for the needs of former slaves so that eventually they could become independent and self-sufficient and (2) to gain black political support for the Republican party. The bureau continued to operate until 1872. Its most lasting achievement was founding and helping Negro colleges.

In April 1865 Lincoln said, "I will hang no rebels." And he remained firm in his commitment to "reconstruct" the South, with the hope that it would be a better place for all its citizens. Lincoln was very serious about this obligation to uphold the Constitution. There were others in Congress, however, who

The Freedmen's Bureau gave assistance to former slaves and served as a base of the Republican party to gain black support.

Thaddeus Stevens

wanted to treat the South like a defeated province. United States Representative Thaddeus Stevens, a Republican from Pennsylvania, called for punitive action against the South. He proposed that large southern plantations be confiscated and divided into small farms. Each slave was to be assigned, for rental, not more than forty acres. At the end of three years, they could buy the farm. The proposition was adopted, and the Freedmen's Bureau was put in charge of assigning the plots of land. Even today, some black families still hold deeds to property that was secured during this period.

President Lincoln's plan called for moderation toward the South without compromising his efforts to fully emancipate the black people. However, Lincoln was assassinated before he could put his plans into work.

The Death of Abraham Lincoln

On April 14, 1865, Abraham Lincoln attended a performance in Ford's Theater in Washington, D.C. Seated in a large black walnut rocker placed there for his comfort, President Lincoln watched Laura Keene perform. John Wilkes Booth came up behind the president and shot him. A few hours later Abraham Lincoln was pronounced dead.

The nation was both shocked and grieved by the death of its president. But none took his death more personally than did the four million former slaves who called Lincoln the Great Emancipator. For them Abraham Lincoln stood for all that was right and decent in human behavior. In black communities from rural Georgia to upstate New York, people gathered quietly to mourn a person who had helped them more than any other had ever dared. The songs of rejoicing changed to songs of mourning. Blacks speculated about how Lincoln's death would affect their struggle for equality. Great hopes were becoming great fears. The

President Lincoln was shot by John Wilkes Booth while he was attending a play at Ford's Theatre in Washington, D.C.

blacks did not know if Congress, without Lincoln, would uphold the rights of freed slaves. And those fears were not unfounded. Some leaders began to worry about setbacks in the progress made since emancipation. They worried about the future, and with reason.

Black leaders were not invited to participate in Lincoln's funeral services. After protests, a few black leaders were admitted, but they had to march in the back of the funeral procession. It was an omen of things yet to come.

Another concern in the black community was Vice-President Andrew Johnson, the new president. What was this former tailor from Tennessee going to do to advance the cause of freedom, justice, and rights? Fears continued to mount. Nobody knew what to expect.

Congress passed the second Freedmen's Bureau Act. President Johnson vetoed the act. Instead he called for a vote to readmit southern states to Congress. Led by radical Republicans, it was overwhelmingly defeated 109 to 10 in the House and 29 to 18 in the Senate. This began the long battle between President Johnson and Congress, one led by Reconstruction leaders Charles Sumner and Thaddeus Stevens, who both bitterly opposed reconciliation with the South.

Charles Sumner

Black convicts, who were arrested for a variety of reasons, provided cheap labor.

THE BLACK CODES

Some Southern states boldly passed new black codes designed to impede the social, political, and economic progress of former slaves. The new codes were based on the black codes that had been written to restrict slaves in the early 1800s. Just before Congress met at the end of 1865, Mississippi passed a series of these black codes. Interracial marriage, for example, was a felony that was punishable by death. Another code prevented former slaves from owning or renting land outside an incorporated town. That was designed to undermine the "forty acres" plan. South Carolina passed a law that required black men to "be in the employ of a reputable white person" or be arrested for vagrancy. That discouraged any economic or educational progress among young black males. Once arrested for vagrancy, black males were tried, convicted, and sentenced to serve in farm camps that supplied cheap labor for white-owned farms and businesses. Diehard racists were determined to "keep things the way they were," and it was working.

Life as a sharecropper was almost as bad as slavery.

Sharecropping was the South's response to the Thirteenth Amendment. In theory the sharecropping concept appeared fair and reasonable. A poor man agreed to work the land of a landowner. At the end of the harvest, the landowner and the farmer were supposed to divide the profits. In practice, though, this did not always happen.

Southerners cannot be blamed for inventing the system, just as they did not invent slavery. But the way that sharecropping dehumanized people and stripped them of their basic human rights made it a deplorable system in the South. Here is how it worked.

Southern planters had land, but no cash or credit; the blacks had no land, and most had only agricultural skills. Black farmers (and many poor white farmers and, later, other minorities) agreed to work small portions of land for landowners. The landowner supplied seeds, tools, food, and clothing to the sharecropper on credit, and sometimes at extremely high costs. But the sharecropper could not get credit anywhere else. The landowner also provided a mule and housing—usually a run-down shack—for which he also charged rent.

After the harvest was over and the crop was sold by the landowner, he took his half, which usually was not much. From the sharecropper's half he deducted all rents, fees, and other charges. That usually left the sharecropper with little or no profit. It was not uncommon for sharecroppers to end up owing the landowner. Year after year the debt got larger and both the landowner and tenant farmer poorer and poorer.

If the farmer tried to leave or to seek help, the landowner had him arrested and, of course, sentenced to work on the same farm he was trying to flee. If the poor farmer stood up for his rights, he was often beaten or killed.

The Joint Committee of Fifteen

THE RADICAL CONGRESS

The Freedmen's Bureau commissioners reported these miscarriages of justice to the authorities in Washington. Southern leaders, however, continued to argue that the Freedmen's Bureau was oppressive. They made it clear that they were going to resist any changes forced on them by "radicals." Congress responded angrily. When Congress met at the end of 1865, southern state members were not seated. The Republican majority formed the Joint Committee of Fifteen on Reconstruction. Two principal leaders in the "radical" Congress were Senator Charles Sumner from Massachusetts and Representative Thaddeus Stevens from

Pennsylvania. Sumner and Stevens took the leadership in submitting "rights" legislation to counter southern resistance and the black codes. But President Johnson did not always agree with Congress.

ANDREW JOHNSON

PRESIDENT ANDREW JOHNSON VERSUS CONGRESS

Congress extended the duration of the Freedmen's Bureau from one to five years and expanded its powers. A bill was introduced that gave the bureau the authority to provide educational opportunities for black children and adults, to defend people when their rights were violated, and to protect the civil rights of blacks in southern states. Civil rights were defined as "any of the civil rights or immunities belonging to white persons, including the rights to make and enforce contracts, to sue, be parties and give evidence, to inherit, purchase, lease, sell, hold and convey real personal property, and to have full and equal benefits of all laws and proceedings for the security of person and estate, including the constitutional right of bearing arms."

A cartoon showing President Andrew Johnson vetoing the bill to protect civil rights of blacks

President Johnson vetoed the bill. He argued that the Constitution did not warrant it and that the term "civil rights" had not been clearly defined. He called for moderation and warned that the passage of such a bill would keep the nation divided.

In addition, President Johnson objected to the sections regarding education and housing. He felt that education and housing were within the states' jurisdiction, not the federal government's. In his opinion, black men were free; it was up to them to find their own schools, to build their own houses, and to make their own way. He gave no clue as to where former slaves were going to get the resources to do these things. They had been

slaves for the better part of two centuries. They had been free for less than two years. With limited opportunities, no money, and nobody willing to give them either, failure was a certainty. It was obvious that they needed help. Even though Johnson knew about the black codes, he held his position, repeating that the freedmen did not need the protections spelled out in the bill.

The Civil Rights Act of 1866 and the Fourteenth Amendment

On March 13, 1866, Congress passed an act entitled "An Act to Protect All Persons in the United States in Their Civil Rights, and Furnish the Means of Their Vindication." It granted that all persons born in the United States were citizens with full rights and privileges of citizenship as provided in the Constitution.

Johnson vetoed the bill, arguing that the bill made citizens of the Chinese on the Pacific coast, Mexicans who lived within the United States border, Gypsies (Eastern Europeans), and Indians.

President Johnson asked, "[Was] it sound policy to make all those colored peoples citizens?"

Congress answered by passing the bill over his veto by an overwhelming margin. Two months after the Civil Rights Act became law, the Senate passed the Fourteenth Amendment to the Constitution. On June 13, 1866, the amendment was passed in the House. It simply stated,

> THE FOURTEENTH AMENDMENT, Section 1: All persons born or naturalized in the United States and subject to the jurisdiction thereof, are citizens of the United States and of the State wherein they reside. No State shall make or enforce any law which shall abridge the privileges or immunities of citizens of the United States; nor shall any State deprive any person of life, liberty or property, without due process of law; nor deny to any person within its jurisdiction the equal protection of the laws.

The Reconstruction Act

The Fourteenth Amendment was declared a lawful part of the Constitution in 1868. However, the amendment's legality was later questioned from time to time because of the way it was ratified. Confederate states were not permitted to vote for or against the amendment's ratification. Tennessee was the only southern state to sign it without force.

Most southern states did not sign the Fourteenth Amendment, so the committee headed by Thaddeus Stevens won Congressional approval for the Reconstruction Act on March 2, 1867. This act prohibited southern participation in Congress until the states ratified the amendment and held conventions to ratify new state constitutions. Then the South was divided into five military districts that were controlled by martial law.

Southern resentment against the Fourteenth Amendment and

Race riot in Memphis, Tennessee

the Reconstruction Act ran high. Race riots broke out in Memphis and New Orleans. There was widespread uncontrollable violence. Mobs broke into homes and burned, beat, and killed blacks.

Thaddeus Stevens gives the closing speech on President Johnson's impeachment.

Andrew Johnson's Impeachment

President Johnson had more opponents in Congress than he had friends. Blinded by their mistrust of President Johnson, his foes failed to give his administration credit for having done anything worthy of praise. However, under the Johnson administration, William Henry Seward, then secretary of state, purchased Alaska from the Russians for $7.2 million—about three cents per acre. Seward's Folly, as it was called, turned out to be one of the best peaceful acquisitions of land since the Louisiana Purchase. At the time, however, Johnson's critics lampooned him for buying a big lump of "Russian ice."

Congress neither respected nor trusted Johnson's position on Reconstruction. To restrict his power Congress passed the Tenure of Office Act in 1867. It forbade President Johnson to dismiss a cabinet officer without approval of Congress. In a direct challenge, Johnson asked for the resignation of Edwin Stanton, the secretary of war. And the impeachment proceedings began.

Congressman Thaddeus Stevens, Johnson's most bitter political enemy, was very ill, but he was helped into the House of Representatives so he could be given the "honor" of delivering the impeachment resolution to the House in February 1868. President Johnson's defense attorney was Henry Stanberry, the former attorney general. American citizens were shocked that their president was on trial.

Evidence was given in lengthy speeches that were full of bitter eloquence and patriotic rhetoric. Johnson was impeached in the House of Representatives but was acquitted in the Senate by one vote. Henry Stanberry was given credit for saving President Johnson and the high office of the presidency.

Although Johnson was allowed to serve out the last few months of his term, he was ineffective as a leader. Not long after the impeachment trial, Thaddeus Stevens died. Congressman Benjamin Butler of Massachusetts became the strongest supporter of Reconstruction in the style of Stevens.

The impeachment trial had embarrassed the presidency, but it benefited the Reconstructionists. The trial sent a clear message to future officials that the "Reconstruction Congress" did not sympathize with those who wanted to hurriedly reconcile with the South. Before the South was to be readmitted, leaders wanted to put key civil rights legislation in place. But for the moment they had to elect a president who would work with them.

President Ulysses S. Grant

GRANT AND RECONSTRUCTION

The 1868 Election

At the Republican convention in May 1868, the platform continued to attack Andrew Johnson, thus setting the tone for the general election:

> We profoundly deplore the untimely and tragic death of Abraham Lincoln, and regret the accession of Andrew Johnson to the Presidency, who has acted treacherously to the people who elected him and the cause he was pledged to support . . . and has been justly impeached for high crimes and misdemeanors, and properly pronounced guilty thereof by the vote of thirty-five senators.

The Democrats argued that the Republican party was responsible for keeping the Union divided:

> We arraign the Radical party [the Republican party] for its disregard of right, and the unparalleled oppression and tyranny which have marked its career.

Ku Klux Klan members in their disguises

> Instead of restoring the Union, it has, so far as in its power, dissolved
> it, and subjected ten States, in time of profound peace, to military
> despotism and negro supremacy.

The Reconstructionists got what they wanted. General Ulysses
S. Grant, the hero of the Civil War, was elected president of the
United States. Civil rights legislation flourished, from 1869 to
1875, during his two terms.

The Fifteenth Amendment and the Civil Rights Act of 1870

The Fifteenth Amendment guarantees that "the right of citizens
of the United States to vote shall not be denied or abridged by the
United States or by any State on account of race, color or previous
conditions of servitude." Congress passed the Fifteenth
Amendment in 1869, giving the right to vote to black men only.
Black and white women were excluded.

In response to the civil rights legislation that was passed to help
guarantee and provide black citizenship, the Ku Klux Klan and
other radical organizations went on a rampage. Blacks who tried

to exercise their rights were attacked and often killed. Black homes were burned, as were schools and churches. Any whites who supported the black man's right to vote were given the same treatment. Klan activities were so violent and widespread that President Grant sent additional troops into the South to keep the peace and to make sure that blacks and their white supporters were allowed to register and vote. But the Klan never gave up its resistance against racial equality.

WOMEN REACT TO THE FIFTEENTH AMENDMENT

Women had traditionally supported the abolition of slavery and had been among the strongest supporters of civil rights. However, when the Fifteenth Amendment was passed and former slaves were given the right to vote before white women, there was deep resentment. Julia Ward Howe declared the sentiments of most suffragists of that time. She said that seeing black men governing over white women "seemed to me intolerable tyranny."

Since the Fourteenth Amendment gave women citizens' status and since all citizens were supposed to be able to vote, Susan B. Anthony, the leading suffragist at the time and president of the American Equal Rights Association, registered and voted in the 1872 presidential election. She was arrested but used the opportunity to deliver her famous speech, which began with the question, "Is it a Crime for a United States Citizen to Vote?"

Anthony refused to pay the $100 fine, and for obvious reasons she was not jailed. The judge reasoned, and rightly so, that Anthony would have appealed the case and taken it all the way to the Supreme Court. She was denied that chance.

However, another suffragist did fight her "right-to-vote case" to

Julia Ward Howe   *Susan B. Anthony*

the Supreme Court. In the *Minor v. Happersett* case, the all-male Supreme Court ruled that the Constitution "does not confer the right of suffrage upon anyone, and that the constitutions and laws of the several states which commit that important trust to men alone are not necessarily void."

The Court essentially gave states the right to set voting regulations. Although it was not the intent at the time, this case was used later to take the vote away from blacks.

CARPETBAGGERS AND SCALAWAGS

Southerners were furious about the "occupation troops" in their cities and the steady stream of northern whites, many under church sponsorship, who came there. Both groups were considered intruders.

The soldiers were sent by the government to keep peace. The internal missionaries came legitimately to help former slaves adjust to life as a free people. But there were some people who took advantage of the situation to make a profit at the expense of others. These unscrupulous men—mostly from the North—were known as carpetbaggers, named after the luggage they carried. Southerners who sympathized with them were called scalawags.

Carpetbaggers and scalawags were opportunists, buying land and goods at low prices and selling them at high prices. These people exploited both blacks and whites for personal gain.

Needing someone to blame for their personal losses and for the hardships that followed the war, whites heaped all their frustrations and anger on the carpetbaggers and scalawags. All Northerners were lumped together—the good and the bad—and unfairly labeled carpetbaggers. Any southern white who supported a black for any reason—right or wrong—was held in contempt and unjustly labeled a scalawag or a "nigger lover." In the Southerners' minds, carpetbaggers were representative of all Northerners and the Radical party, the Republicans.

THE RISE OF WHITE SUPREMACY

Congress was at work trying to write laws that would protect the rights of all American citizens. But laws must be written from

Whipping a black girl in North Carolina

the hearts and minds of the people, otherwise they are little more than "paper rights."

Pulaski, Tennessee—1866

As Southerners grew angrier, their anger turned to violence. Six Confederate officers formed the Invisible Empire of the South, a secret organization meant to protect the South from "niggers and nigger lovers." The organization later became known as the Ku Klux Klan.

During the day these men were merchants, farmers, judges, businessmen, laborers, grandfathers, fathers, and sons. At night these same law-abiding citizens covered their faces with hoods and rode throughout the countryside taking the law into their own hands. They were the judge, jury, and hangman.

Their early victims were blacks. Later, Jews, Catholics, and "foreigners" were added to their hate list. The burning cross was the Klan's calling card. Beatings, tar and featherings, burnings, lynchings, and other brutal murders were the Klan's brand of punishment. Their primary goal was to "keep America free for the white man."

During the 1867 initiation of new members into the Knights of the White Camellia (another white supremacist secret organization from New Orleans), the supreme commander asked the following questions.

1. Do you belong to the white race? (I do.)
2. Did you ever marry any woman who did not, or does not, belong to the white race? (No.)
3. Do you promise never to marry any woman but one who belongs to the white race? (I do.)
4. Do you believe in the superiority of your race? (I do.)
5. Will you promise never to vote for anyone for any office of honor, profit or trust who does not belong to your race? (I do.)

Five more questions were asked during the initiation. They were meant to test the candidates' attitudes. If all the answers satisfied the supreme commander, the candidates could become members of the group. Then an oath was taken that bound the new members to secrecy.

Not all white Southerners approved of the Klan and the other terrorist groups. But they were often intimidated into conforming. They either participated in the actions of the groups or they were silent. The seed was planted and the tree grew, but its fruit was bitter and rotten.

Some native-born Protestant Americans belonged to the Know-Nothing party, an organization that was anti-immigrant and anti-Catholic.

BLACKS' GROWTH DURING RECONSTRUCTION

When the Fifteenth Amendment was passed, the word *freedom* took on a new meaning for blacks. Once again there was great rejoicing and sounds of gladness coming from black voices. Black voters meant that blacks were participating in government. Hope blossomed again.

There was a spirit of progress emerging out of impoverished black communities. Black people were not satisfied with the drudgery of cotton fields. Northern blacks, who had never been slaves, had not been convinced that they were inferior beings. The physical and mental chains that had kept their southern brothers in bondage could not hold them. All the efforts to impede their progress seemed to make them more determined to go on.

Through the efforts of the Freedmen's Bureau, blacks were building schools, churches, and small businesses. Free men, treated fairly and with the right to vote, did not need handouts but rather a helping hand to pull themselves up. Building on the individual efforts of a few, a new generation of young blacks slowly advanced themselves in all walks of life.

A dozen black colleges and manual trade institutions were founded during this time: Hampton Institute in Virginia, Morehouse in Georgia, Howard in Washington, D.C., and Fisk in Tennessee. White teachers came to the South, opened schools, and trained other teachers. Ministers and businessmen helped with voter registration and job development. Some of those church- and government-sponsored schools and institutions are still in existence today and carry the names of Reconstruction leaders: Stevens, Sumner, Butler, and Grant.

With better educational opportunities, young black men became interested in holding public office; and with the right to vote,

Students at Hampton Institute learning the printing trade

Julia Hayden was a seventeen-year-old schoolteacher who was in charge of a school in western Tennessee. She was one of the many black teachers murdered to prevent the education of the black race.

Voting in Richmond, Virginia in 1871

many blacks were elected to positions of power on the local, state, and national levels. White Southerners angrily denounced black suffrage as unjust punishment. There were more than a few Northerners who agreed with them. Opponents of black suffrage argued that "slaves were not ready to be responsible voters." Advocates countered, "If not now, when?"

The southern political structure was threatened, so Southerners attacked, using every bit of energy to try to undermine the Fifteenth Amendment so they could stay in power. One way they were able to rally support was to dredge up old fears and prejudices that were born out of ignorance. Politicians warned that blacks were going to take over the land, make the whites servants, and marry their daughters. All this was going to happen because blacks could vote.

In many counties former slaves outnumbered white registered voters, so there was bound to be a shift in power. Blacks successfully elected candidates to public office between 1870 and 1876, but there was no great takeover, nor was one attempted.

Blacks who served in the United States Senate and the House of Representatives during the period from 1869 to 1873. They were from Mississippi, South Carolina, Georgia, Florida, and Alabama.

During Reconstruction, only seventeen black men served in the United States Congress—men like Blanche K. Bruce and Hiram R. Revels from Mississippi and Robert Smalls, a Civil War hero.

Attempts were made to discredit black Reconstruction officeholders by labeling them illiterate, ignorant, incompetent, and pawns of carpetbaggers. But without exception, blacks who served in Congress were described as well educated, well informed, and respectable in all ways. Throughout the United States and the South, local politicians tended to be products of their communities. They ranged from highly qualified to totally incompetent. Race or color did not seem to make much difference.

Another tactic of the southern political establishment was to question the legitimacy of black elected officials. That is what happened to Representative Henry M. Turner in 1868, when he was elected to the Georgia House of Representatives. Even though he had been educated in the North as a minister and had served as a Union army chaplain during the Civil War, his qualifications to hold office were challenged.

After the war Turner stayed in the South and worked for the African Methodist Episcopal Church, helping to build schools and churches for nearly three years before seeking office. Yet his two-year residency requirement was questioned. Turner delivered a six-hour speech to the legislative body, defending his right to be seated. His words are a matter of record:

Mr. Speaker: Before proceeding to argue this question upon its intrinsic merits, I wish the members of this House to understand the position I take. I hold that I am a member of this body. Therefore, sir, I shall neither fawn or cringe before any party, nor stoop to beg them for my rights. Some of my colored fellow members, in the course of their remarks, took occasion to appeal to the sympathies of Members on the opposite side . . . It reminds me very much, sir, of slaves begging under the lash. I am here to demand my rights, and to hurl thunderbolts at the men who would dare to cross the threshold of my manhood. . . . They question my right to a seat in this body, to represent the people whose legal votes elected me. This objection, sir, is an unheard of monopoly of power. No analogy can be found for it, except it be the case of a man who should go into my house, take possession of my wife and children, and then tell me to walk out. I stand very much in the position of a criminal before your bar, because I dare to be the exponent of the views of those who sent me here. . . . The great question, sir, is this: Am I a man? If I am such, I claim the rights of a man. . . .

Henry M. Turner

Turner was seated and served his term. He is only one example of a black leader during the Reconstruction period. Later generations were led to believe that all black elected officials of this period were buffoons, but this was not true.

Just as it was difficult for the black officeholder, it was doubly hard for the voter. When intimidation, deceit, and threats did not work, violence was used to stop blacks from voting, usually under cover of darkness.

William Coleman from Macon, Georgia, described what the Klan did to him after he voted:

> I saw men out there standing with horns and faces on all of them. . . . They told me they rode from Shiloh to kill me. . . .[After a terrible beating by the Klansmen] they left me there for dead, and what it was done for was because I was a radical, and I didn't deny my profession anywhere and I never will. I never will vote that conservative [Democratic] ticket if I die.

Cartoons showing some of the violence inflicted on blacks in the 1860s and 1870s

"ONE VOTE LESS."—*Richmond Whig.*

"IN SELF-DEFENSE."

SOUTHERN CHIV. "Ef I hadn't-er killed you, you would hev growed up to rule me."

THE CIVIL RIGHTS ACT OF 1875

Charles Sumner—a United States senator from Massachusetts and a leading civil rights advocate—introduced the Civil Rights Bill, but he died before it was enacted on March 1, 1875. Its official title was "An Act to Protect All Citizens in Their Civil and Legal Rights." It began with this clause:

> Whereas, it is essential to just government we recognize the equality of all men before the law, and hold that it is the duty of government in its dealings with the people to mete out equal and exact justice to all of whatever nationality, race, color, or persuasion, religious or political; and it being the appropriate object of legislation to enact great fundamental principles of law

The statement was followed by the first section, which spelled out three basic principles:

1. All persons were entitled to "full and equal enjoyment of the accommodations . . . and privileges of inns, public conveyances, . . . theaters, and other places of public amusement . . . regardless of previous condition of servitude."

2. All persons, regardless of race or color, were to be allowed to serve on juries in all court systems in the country.

3. The federal courts supported the two principles above. Any person found guilty of denying a person his civil rights was guilty and could be punished.

The Civil Rights Act of 1875 was the last Reconstruction legislation that was enacted. For ten years or more it had been the intent of Congress to change the status of the black man from a slave to a free citizen and to provide and defend his rights by law.

Reconstructionists believed that, when former slaves were fully and equally protected under the law, they could work toward personal and economic security—each man to his own ability. By the end of 1875 there was reason to believe that this goal was attainable.

Frederick Douglass, a great black leader before and after the Civil War, said that blacks should not despair. ''There is hope for a people when their laws are righteous, whether for the moment they conform to their requirements or not.''

The future of blacks in America had been well protected by national law. But even as the Civil Rights Act was being debated, States' Righters were taking measures at the state level to circumvent the law and to make a mockery of the Constitution.

Frederick Douglass, and a group of blacks from Washington, D.C., pay their respects to the late Senator Charles Sumner, who was a leading civil rights advocate.

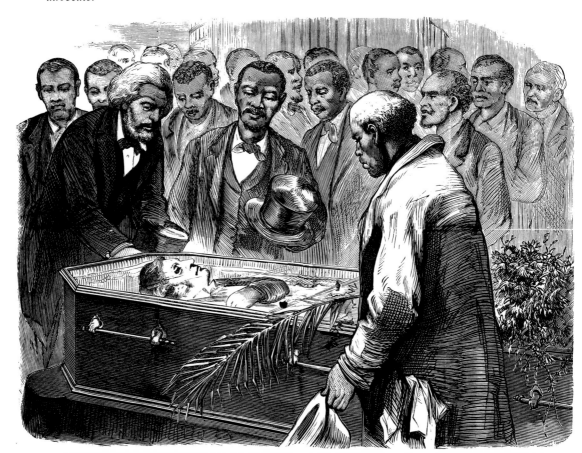

Although blacks were free, they did not fare well, as depicted (above) in a cartoon of 1877 and in the photograph (right) showing an interracial tenement in New York at the turn of the century.

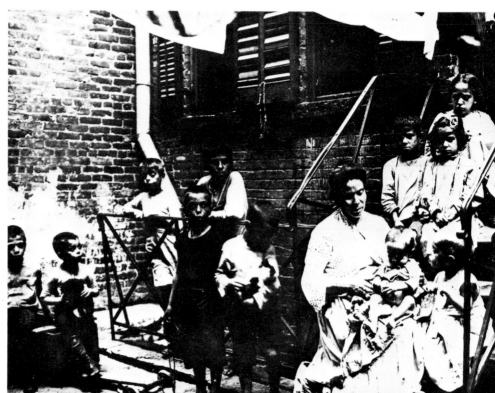

TIME LINE 1876-1900

1876   The end of the Reconstruction Centennial Celebration and the beginning of the Industrial Revolution

1877   Troops removed from the South; state enactment of Jim Crow laws; Rutherford B. Hayes wins presidency by promising to remove federal troops from the South

1879   Exodus of blacks from the South

1880   Large Eastern European immigration

1882   First restrictions on immigration passed, limiting Chinese entry into the United States

1883   Civil Rights Act of 1875 declared unconstitutional

1886   Statue of Liberty unveiled

1894   Defeat of Apache Indians in the Southwest

1895   Death of Frederick Douglass; Booker T. Washington's Atlanta Compromise Speech

1896   *Plessy v. Ferguson* case: U.S. Supreme Court rules that "separate but equal" public accommodations are legal

1898   Spanish-American War—Theodore Roosevelt the hero

1900   Disenfranchisement of the blacks and other minorities in the South and many border states

1876-1900

RECONSTRUCTION ENDS

In 1872 the Amnesty Bill pardoned all Southerners, and by 1875 all the southern states had been readmitted to Congress. Historians mark the 1876 election year as the unofficial end of Reconstruction.

President Grant was described as "abounding in kindness and generosity." But most historians also agree that he was a far better general than he was a president. However, during his administration very important civil rights legislation was passed. The full effect of that legislation would not be realized until many years later. Among blacks Grant was a hero, second only to Lincoln. So in 1872, when Grant ran for a second term, black voters gave him their full support—and he won.

Attitudes had changed by 1876, and members in both parties were moving toward more moderate positions. The Radical party had been losing members since the 1870s because of legislation that some considered too liberal and because of the widespread corruption in Grant's administration. Stevens and Sumner were dead. Younger leaders, who were more willing to compromise, took over the party. Democrats and Republicans were looking for issues on which they could agree instead of disagree.

Blacks considered President Grant second only to Lincoln.

The Election of 1876

Eighteen seventy-six marked the first time that all thirty-five states were seated in Congress since 1860, and it was an election year. Democrats and Republicans were looking for strong presidential candidates to represent their party platforms. Rutherford B. Hayes, a Republican from Ohio, and Samuel J. Tilden, a Democrat from New York, were the presidential candidates. Southern leaders were determined that the black vote would not sway another election. This decision resulted in the disgraceful election of 1876, which stands on record as being the most corrupt election held in American history. Here is what happened.

"Free" elections in 1876

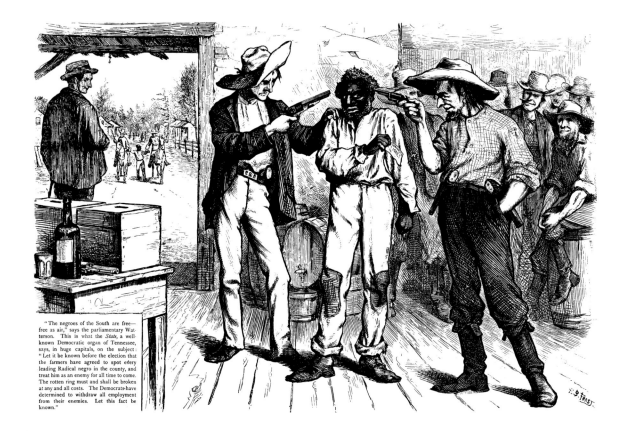

"The negroes of the South are free—free as air," says the parliamentary Watterson. This is what the *State*, a well-known Democratic organ of Tennessee, says, in huge capitals, on the subject : "Let it be known before the election that the farmers have agreed to spot every leading Radical negro in the county, and treat him as an enemy for all time to come. The rotten ring must and shall be broken at any and all costs. The Democrats have determined to withdraw all employment from their enemies. Let this fact be known."

Private voting booths were not used at the time, so citizens in the South who came to vote did so in public and under the watchful eye of the Klan. If a person did not vote the "right way," his ballot was changed, "lost," or sometimes torn up. Houses were burned to frighten potential voters, and unchecked violence occurred throughout the region. Even the military troops who were in the South to keep peace were attacked by angry mobs.

Ballot boxes were destroyed, blacks were driven away from voting places by hooded Klansmen, and voting places were hidden or moved at the last minute. Those who came to vote even though they were threatened were arrested for some minor reason just before they tried to vote.

In South Carolina a voting official told his workers:

> Never threaten a man individually. If he deserves to be threatened, the necessities of the times require that he should die. A dead Radical is harmless—a threatened Radical or one driven off by threats from the scene of his operations is often troublesome, sometimes dangerous.

The Bargain of 1877

The climax of the 1876 election came when neither Hayes nor Tilden received enough electoral votes to claim a victory. Clearly, Tilden had won the popular vote, which earned him 184 electoral votes. He needed one more electoral vote to win the presidency. Hayes had 165 electoral votes and needed twenty more to win.

The returns from four states were still outstanding. These were Oregon and three southern states, Louisiana, Florida, and South Carolina. Their combined electoral votes numbered twenty. Oregon went to Hayes. In the meantime the three southern states sent in two different sets of returns. An electoral commission, composed of seven Democrats and eight Republicans, was called

The inauguration of Rutherford B. Hayes in 1877

upon to settle the matter. The commission returned an 8 to 7 verdict in favor of Hayes, giving him the twenty electoral votes he needed to win.

Hayes had agreed to withdraw the last of the federal troops that still remained in Louisiana, Florida, and South Carolina in exchange for the crucial votes he needed. It was later called "The Bargain of 1877." Reconstruction had ended.

PRESIDENT HAYES AND STATES' RIGHTS

From the beginning President Hayes sent a clear message to the South that the federal government was no longer interested in pushing for more civil rights legislation. To further clarify his position, President Hayes held up his end of the election bargain and immediately pulled out the last of the federal troops in the southern states.

Black leaders expressed their alarm. They felt betrayed. President Hayes assured blacks that their fears were unfounded, and he accused them of overreacting. President Hayes refused to accept reports of Klan terror, voting violations, beatings, burnings, and lynchings. He called for reconciliation between the races and made a "goodwill" tour throughout the South. Black hopes for a reconstructed South were shattered.

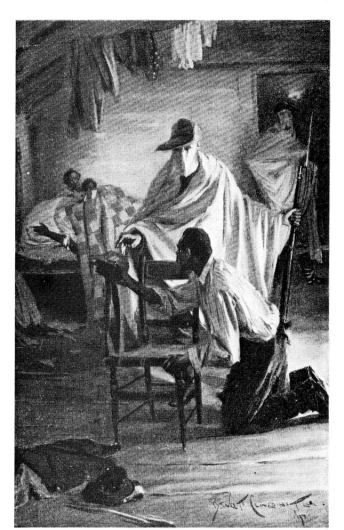

Members of the Ku Klux Klan were described as "awful forms wrapped like ghosts in winding sheets."

Actually, Hayes's attitude was a reflection of the time. The nation was industrializing and becoming more internationally recognized as an industrial power. There had been a cooling-off period since the Civil War, and people were calling for unity and reconciliation between the North and the South. Interest in the plight of blacks (and other minorities) was out of vogue. When black leaders pleaded for help, they often were asked, "What more do you people want?" The answer was so obvious that among blacks the question was held in contempt. Within a few short years, blacks would be second-class citizens in the United States.

RIGHTS UNDER ATTACK

In many southern towns blacks were a majority. Their votes made a big difference in election outcomes. Whites wanted to recapture their all-white power structure by disenfranchising blacks. Intimidation and manipulation had not stopped blacks from voting in large numbers and neither had Klan terror. White southern leaders looked for ways that could forfeit black Americans' voting rights quickly, permanently, and legally.

White supremacists were emboldened by the recent changes. The federal soldiers were gone; the Hayes administration was looking for other ways, and opinion regarding civil rights was, at best, lukewarm. So they enacted state legislation that was blatantly unconstitutional. The first of these were "poll taxes."

Poll Taxes

Throughout the South, poll taxes were instituted to stop blacks from voting. The idea of poll taxes was not new. New Hampshire had charged a voting tax in 1776. Although the fee was not more than $1.50, all kinds of unreasonable requirements were attached to the taxing procedure.

For example, to vote in one southern county, the poll tax had to be presented to officials months in advance on an unpublished date. Black voters often learned that their receipts, being written on blue instead of pink paper, disqualified them as voters. These are just two examples of the legal trickery that was used to disenfranchise black Americans.

Not all Southerners took part in or even approved of this blatant obstruction of justice. But if they spoke out, they became victims of Klan attacks. They became outcasts, their families were harassed, and sometimes they were beaten and killed.

Literacy Tests and the Grandfather Clause

Literacy tests were used to test a person's competency to vote. In theory it sounded reasonable, and it was generally agreed that voters should be responsible people. But the questions that were asked on the voting test were hardly reasonable or responsible. They included questions like, How many angels can dance on the head of a pin? How far is far? How long is forever? How many bubbles in a soap bar? How high is up? Men who had earned college degrees were declared unqualified to vote because they could not pass a literacy test.

Sometimes these schemes backfired. Black people were just as determined to hold onto their rights, even though those rights were slipping away one by one. They fought back as best they could.

A favorite literacy test question was to ask the prospective voter to recite the Constitution of the United States. More than a few voting officials were surprised when a black man recited the

Constitution word for word. That is how badly some people wanted to vote. However, any person who dared to defy the system in this way usually got a visit from the Klan. They made sure the "smart nigger" did not get to vote—ever!

A number of states passed the grandfather clause, which stated that no person who had voted before 1867 or who had relatives who had voted needed to take the literacy test. Of course, no blacks had voted before 1867, so they were required to take the literacy test, and they were sure to fail—or to wish they had.

As segregation laws passed one by one in state after state, Rutherford B. Hayes and the new Congress turned their heads.

Black leaders were told to seek help on the state level. The federal government had "been partial to the Freedmen long enough."

THE CENTENNIAL

It was a good year—1876! Colorado became a state, the National Baseball League was founded, and America celebrated its one-hundredth birthday.

Philadelphia hosted the Centennial Exposition, which has been called the dawning of the Industrial Revolution. Inventions such as Alexander Graham Bell's telephone, C. L. Sholes's typewriter, and Eastman's Kodak camera were on display. Soon these prototypes were used to create new industries and factory jobs. America was on the move.

The sewing machine would change the clothing industry. Railroads would replace river transportation. Electricity instead of gaslights would light America's streets. Old jobs such as lamplighting would die out, but new jobs involving telephone operators and typists would be created. Americans were on the move.

Horace Greeley's advice—"Go West, young man, go West"—caught on. St. Louis, Missouri, was named the Gateway to the West, and in the late 1870s Easterners flocked there with hope and anticipation. Some with carefree abandon and others with well-planned reason decided to follow the Oregon Trail to Oregon or the Santa Fe Trail to the great Southwest. Some would make it; some would not.

Every day wagon trains left St. Louis filled with adventurers, speculators, businessmen, farmers, those looking for a fresh beginning, and those searching for something better. Included in this group of pioneers were southern blacks.

Chinese emigrated to the American Northwest during the end of the nineteenth century. There were riots. In 1885, many Chinese were massacred in Rock Springs, Wyoming.

MIGRATION AND IMMIGRATION

During the last quarter of the nineteenth century, there was a mass movement of people throughout the world. Thousands of Europeans and Asians left their homelands to seek new homes and a new way of life in America. At the same time, Americans were leaving the Northeast and settling lands in the northwest and southwest portions of the country. Still another exodus was taking place in the South.

The Black Exodus

As life became more restrictive in the South, blacks abandoned their homes. Like their runaway slave ancestors—the fed-up sharecroppers—they chose to follow the North Star to a better place. One by one, blacks slipped away, very often a few steps ahead of the sheriff and his bloodhounds. Instead of southern whites rejoicing over the exodus, they tried to stop it. The idea was not to drive blacks away but to keep them in the South to supply cheap labor. Many blacks did leave the South during this period, but many more chose to stay. It was home.

In the industrial North black families were able to find some relief from the endless oppression and senseless cruelty. They found jobs in factories and mills. And even though housing and educational opportunities remained minimal, the city black felt a bit more privileged than did his country cousin.

Many blacks settled in Arkansas, Louisiana, and Texas, while a few moved to the new promised land beyond the Mississippi River. Here was freedom and free land—every opportunity a man needed to succeed.

As in other periods in American history, black Americans helped to tame the vast wilderness and to shape its future. White and black families worked together, shared the same hardships, and endured the same suffering and pain until their common dreams were fulfilled. Both their contributions were essential and therefore significant.

Yet when the history books were written, black pioneers were excluded. For years people did not know that there were black cowboys, surveyors, trappers, traders, and scouts. They had never heard of the elite black fighting group known as the Buffalo Soldiers, who were well respected for their bravery and courage.

A Frederic Remington drawing of Buffalo Soldiers in the West

Without fear and intimidation to hamper them out West, blacks opened businesses, bought farms, and built schools, churches, and prosperous communities. For a while many black families thought they had found true freedom. The western frontier was so wondrously big and open that it did not seem possible that small, bigoted ideas would flourish. But racism and prejudice found fertile ground in the West—some of the worst ever.

European Immigration—the First Wave

In the 1880s over 23.5 million foreigners would enter the United States and settle along the eastern seacoast. Sixty percent of those immigrants were peasants from Italy, Russia, Austria, Hungary,

A boardinghouse for immigrants in New York City

Bulgaria, Turkey, Poland, and Greece. They were mostly Catholics and Jews who were fleeing European religious and political persecution.

Soon Eastern cities were bulging. Among the new immigrants, English illiteracy was high and incomes were low. Female heads of households numbered four million. Many immigrant families were forced to rely on their children for added income. Nine- and ten-year-olds took jobs in mines and sweatshops for $1.50 per week. As neighborhoods turned into slums, crime spread—and racial prejudice provided a comfortable scapegoat.

The Eastern European was labeled the problem. Since these people tended to have darker eye, hair, and skin coloring, they were considered inferior to the lighter Anglo-European. Thus the

Ku Klux Klan added Jews, Catholics (mainly because of Italians), and any other foreigners to their hate list.

West Coast Asian Immigrants

During the late 1800s, Chinese were experiencing racism on the West Coast. Over two hundred thousand Chinese workers had come to the United States to help lay the tracks for the transcontinental railroad, which was completed in 1869. The depression of the 1870s caused a shortage of jobs. As a result, there were violent race riots, and the Chinese worker was the victim. West Coast laborers called for Chinese immigrant labor to cease.

An anti-Chinese demonstration in San Francisco in 1880

Denis Kearney addressing the workingmen about the Chinese problem

By 1881 the Workingman's party of California, led by Denis Kearney (himself an Irish immigrant), helped to promote legislation that prohibited the hiring of Chinese. This paved the way for the 1882 federal legislation that suspended the entry of Chinese laborers and that barred foreign-born Chinese from citizenship. In a California legislative report, an unprecedented racist statement was recorded: "The Chinese are inferior to any race God ever made."

Thousands of Chinese returned to China. Others went to Hawaii, and a few remained in the continental United States. Those who stayed had very few rights. They were forced to live in segregated sections of town and to maintain separate schools and businesses. When the Japanese and other Asian people came to the United States at the turn of the century, they experienced similar limitations based solely on racism.

A Mexican family in the Southwest

Mexican-Americans and Native Americans

In the Southwest, after the end of the Mexican War in 1848, many Mexican-Americans settled permanently in the United States. But a majority of Mexican-Americans stayed in the United States primarily to earn enough money to take home to their families who were still living in Mexico. They disregarded border lines and moved freely between the United States and Mexico. They too were victims of racism and were stereotyped as lazy and shiftless. Mexican-Americans, who lived mainly in the Southwest, were tolerated by whites. Some were tolerated because they were useful to wealthy landowners and ranchers. Poor Mexican-Americans provided cheap labor.

A delegation of Indian chiefs in the corridor of the White House, waiting to talk to the president

The Native American was neither liked nor tolerated. Indians were stereotyped either as noble savages capable of doing no wrong or as murderous heathens unfit to live in a civilized world. Neither representation is accurate. Native Americans, like all other humans, are capable of hurting and being hurt, loving and needing love, and fearing and being feared. They wanted what all other Americans wanted—life, liberty, and the pursuit of happiness. But through trickery they lost their homeland, and when they defended their rights, they also lost their freedom.

The Indians had something that everyone wanted—land. The Native American was portrayed as an enemy of the United States. Americans united to fight against them: whites, blacks, immigrants, Northerners, Southerners, the young, and the old. And although they put up a good fight, one by one the tribes were defeated—the Arapaho, the Comanche, the Kiowa, the Apache, the Sioux, the Navaho—and were forced to live on reservations.

Cheyenne Indians going to their reservation

Reservation life was alien to them. The Indians were a nomadic people who had freely roamed the plains, mountains, and deserts. The endless lies that flowed from Washington, the broken treaties, and the vanishing buffalo herds brought an end to their way of life. By 1885 the American Indians were a people without rights, privileges, or freedom in their homeland.

LAWS—CHANGES AND CHALLENGES

Meanwhile debates over voting rights were still under way in Washington. Was voting a right to be granted by states or was it within the power of the federal government? Women had gained the vote in several western states. Wyoming was the first state to grant women the right to vote. Then in 1878 Senator A. A. Sargent introduced the Woman Suffrage Amendment. But women had a long battle before them. The Sargent Bill was introduced and defeated every year until 1920.

As women gained support for their suffrage, black men were losing vital support for theirs, especially, in the courts. The courts ruled that each state was free to set its own voting requirements. Poll taxes and literacy tests were declared legal because they were required of whites as well as blacks. States had the right to compile their own literacy tests. So no federal guidelines were set.

Meanwhile, white supremacist groups continued fighting against equal rights for blacks and other minorities. According to statistics compiled by Ida B. Wells Barnett, an outspoken leader of the antilynch crusade, more blacks were lynched than were legally executed in southern states. In a newspaper article published in the *Independent* on May 16, 1901, Barnett presented startling figures showing that between 1890 and 1899, blacks were being lynched on the average of two per week throughout the South. Very often the only crime the victims had committed was to "look wrong" or "to be sassy."

Occasionally, blacks fought back against a lynch mob, as in the case of Jack Trice from Jacksonville, Florida. The Cleveland *Press Gazette*, on May 30, 1896, reported that Trice's young son had beaten up a white boy whose father was the town marshal. A group of fourteen white men went to the Trice home to "regulate" the boy. When Trice refused to send out his son, the white mob opened fire. Trice shot back, and the first bullet killed the marshal.

Jack Trice killed three whites and wounded two others before he and his son escaped. The vigilante group, with reinforcements, returned to the house. Finding Trice gone, they burned the house down and drove out Trice's aged mother.

Although lynchings, rapes of black women, beatings, and

property destruction were common assaults against black people, black retaliation was uncommon. Laws that had previously protected people and property were being declared unconstitutional.

BLACKS TAKE THE OFFENSIVE

Black people learned quickly that the best way to make their dreams come true was to wake up to the harsh realities that their rights were being taken away from them one by one. They had to fight back, or they would lose everything. Trying to overthrow their oppressor by force was not the answer. Black leadership chose education as a weapon. Another effective weapon was the press.

By 1900 there were about 150 weekly black newspapers being published. The *Pittsburgh Courier,* the *Chicago Defender,* and the *St. Louis Argus* are examples of quality newspapers that were started by blacks and "played key roles in advancing the level of the race's knowledge, pride, and militancy."

T. Thomas Fortune of *New York Age* and William Monroe Trotter, founder of the *Boston Guardian,* were two editors who brought to the public's attention issues that affected black people. Black accomplishments, often unnoticed by the white press, were

*William
Monroe
Trotter*

A group of blacks meeting in the House of Representatives at New Orleans

regular features, and news events were presented in detail. Young artists and writers were given an opportunity to showplace their talents as well.

Black leaders realized they needed to organize so that they could present a unified front when negotiating with the all-white administrations, state and federal. Meetings were frequently held to discuss the various problems that faced their people. In 1883 the National Convention of Colored People was held in Louisville, Kentucky. The black National Baptist Convention and its publishing arm, the National Baptist Publishing House, were also started during this time.

The major point of concern was racism. Race prejudice was no longer contained in the South; it was spreading to points north and west. The trend toward segregation—a forced separation of the races—was growing all over the country.

"The National Negro Convention adopted a constitution and formed an Afro-American League that was meant to be a permanent nonpartisan civil rights organization oriented toward legal redress of grievances." Although the league did not last long, it was the forerunner of the highly successful National Association for the Advancement of Colored People (NAACP).

By the end of the century the first generation of freeborn blacks was living up to what the Freedmen's Bureau had hoped for. Many were college graduates, skilled workers, and responsible citizens. The work of black artists and writers also flourished.

DIFFERENCES IN BLACK LEADERSHIP

Frederick Douglass died in 1895. His death created a void in black leadership. Douglass had been the most influential black person in America. He left black people a legacy of hope:

> We are a hopeful people . . . our belief [is] that prejudice, with all its malign accompaniments, may yet be removed by peaceful means; that, assisted by time and events and the growing enlightenment of both races, the color line will ultimately become harmless.

Frederick Douglass

Douglass's message was prophetic. But black people were looking to the immediate future. Who would take Frederick Douglass's place? The answer came in the person of an Alabama educator named Booker T. Washington.

Booker T. Washington and the Atlanta Compromise

Like Douglass, Booker T. Washington was a former slave who was emancipated by Abraham Lincoln. Washington graduated from college and later founded the Tuskegee Institute in 1881.

In 1895 Washington was asked to deliver a short speech at the Cotton States Exposition in Atlanta, Georgia. He began his speech with a story: There once were two ships that passed each other at sea. The captain of the first ship called that they needed water. The captain of the second ship answered, "Cast down your buckets where you are." Three times the first captain begged for water, and three times the second captain replied, "Cast down

Booker T. Washington (right) in his office at Tuskegee Institute, with his secretary Emmett J. Scott

your buckets where you are." At last the first captain did as he was told, and he pulled up a bucketful of fresh water from the mouth of the Amazon River.

Washington explained the meaning of this story to this mostly white audience. He said that the two ships were like the two races. He encouraged black people to "cast down their buckets" by learning crafts and trades and by becoming good and willing workers. "No race," he said, "can prosper till it learns that there is as much dignity in tilling a field as in writing a poem. It is at the bottom of life we must begin, and not at the top. Nor should we permit our grievances to overshadow our opportunities."

Washington encouraged whites also to "cast down their buckets" by hiring skilled and trustworthy black laborers. He ended, saying, "In all things that are purely social, we can be as separate as the fingers, yet one as the hand in things essential to mutual progress."

When the educator from Alabama finished his speech, which has become known as the Atlanta Compromise, whites gave him a thunderous ovation. He was received afterward with great enthusiasm.

It was not surprising. A black man seemed to be advocating segregation. He seemed to be telling black people that they need not worry about being equal. Immediately, whites proclaimed Booker T. Washington the spokesman for *all* black people. But all black people did not agree with his philosophy, especially W.E.B. DuBois.

W.E.B. DuBois

The same year that Washington made his famous speech, W.E.B. DuBois received his Ph.D. in sociology from Harvard University in Boston. He accepted a teaching position at Atlanta College.

DuBois was sick with anger when he learned that a black man was being lynched in Georgia every three days. In response, he wrote a collection of essays entitled *The Souls of Black Folk*, which has become an American literary classic.

DuBois launched a direct attack on Washington's compromise. "This 'Atlanta Compromise' is by all odds the most notable thing in Mr. Washington's career. The South interpreted it in different ways: the radicals received it as a complete surrender of the demand for civil and political equality; the conservatives, as a generously conceived working basis for mutual understanding. So both approved it, and today its author is certainly the most distinguished Southerner since Jefferson Davis, and the one with the largest personal following.

W.E.B. DuBois was the editor of The Crisis, *the magazine published by the National Association for the Advancement of Colored People.*

"Mr. Washington distinctly asks that black people give up, at least for the present, three things—First, political power. Second, insistence on civil rights. Third, higher education of Negro youth." To the question, What do black people want? DuBois answered with three goals: "(1) The right to vote; (2) Civil equality; [and] (3) The education of youth according to ability."

Washington and DuBois essentially wanted the same things for blacks, but in theory they disagreed about how and when they were to reach these goals. Washington chose conformity and long-suffering patience. DuBois was driven by a sense of immediacy. He called for black people to never let up in their struggle for freedom: "resist . . . agitate . . . resist!"

Whites found it difficult to accept DuBois's quick and direct style; he used the written and spoken language masterfully and had a careful ear when listening. DuBois used assertive language and his superior intellect to persuade and convince people. He was successful and popular among black youths. It was the young who would continue the struggle for freedom and equality—and they did so forcefully.

Washington's communication style was very different. His language was less strident, less judgmental, and he delivered his speeches slower and in a softer tone. His message was never offensive, but it was challenging. White audiences were lulled into believing that he presented no threat. Yet Booker T. Washington was a threat. Under his leadership blacks were able to keep and even to gain support for some of their institutions and causes. And in so doing, they could continue the struggle quietly and unobtrusively while the cause got stronger.

The conflict between Booker T. Washington and W.E.B. DuBois has been analyzed for decades. Who was right? Who was wrong? Both men's opinion and styles were as varied as the people they represented. Black people did not think with a collective brain. It was foolish to think that they did, and it was just as ridiculous to believe that they would all acquiesce to one man's political leadership. Washington had followers, but so did DuBois. Obviously, there was a need for both voices.

TWO STEPS BACKWARD . . .

Plessy V. Ferguson

Homer Plessy was forced to sit in a segregated train car. Plessy challenged the Louisiana railroad for violating his civil rights. The case was heard by the Supreme Court in 1896. The Court, like Congress, had changed from the earlier Reconstruction days. One Southerner, Justice Harlan, was seated on the Supreme Court. The idea of states' rights was increasing in popularity.

All but one justice ruled in favor of the "separate but equal" concept. The decision handed down by Justice Henry B. Brown included a statement made by Justice Joseph P. Bradley from the resolution of a similar case in 1883:

> After giving to these questions all the consideration which their importance demands, we are forced to the conclusion that such an act of refusal has nothing to do with slavery or involuntary servitude, and that if it is violative of any right of the party, his redress is to be sought under the laws of the state; or if those laws are adverse to his rights and do not protect him, his remedy will be found in the corrective legislation which Congress has adopted, or may adopt, for counteracting the effect of State laws or State action prohibited by the Fourteenth Amendment. It would be running the slavery argument into the ground to make it apply to every act of discrimination which a person may see fit to make as to the guests he will entertain, or as to the people he will take into his coach or cab or car, or admit to his concert or theater, or deal with in other matters of intercourse or business.

Justice Joseph P. Bradley

As Justice Brown's conclusion in this landmark case of 1896 agreed completely with that made in the 1883 case, the Supreme Court had armed and entrenched the legal means by which the states might deny any person's civil rights without fear of federal law. Blacks and some whites were outraged, but the Supreme Court had ruled.

Justice Harlan's Dissent

Justice John Harlan was the dissenting judge. He disagreed with his colleagues, saying, "But in view of the Constitution, in the eye of the law, there is in this country no superior, dominant, ruling class of citizens. There is no caste here. Our Constitution is color-

Justice John M. Harlan was the one Southerner on the Supreme Court at the time of Plessy v. Ferguson, *and the only dissenter.*

blind, and neither knows nor tolerates classes among citizens. In respect of civil rights, all citizens are equal before the law. The humblest is the peer of the most powerful. The law regards man as man, and takes no account of his surroundings or of his color when his civil rights as guaranteed by the supreme law of the land are involved. It is, therefore, to be regretted that this high tribunal, the final expositor of the fundamental law of the land, has reached the conclusion that it is competent for a State to regulate the enjoyment by citizens of their civil rights solely upon the basis of race. . . .

"The destinies of the two races, in this country, are indissolubly linked together, and the interests of both require that the common government of all shall not permit the seeds of race hate to be planted under the sanction of law. . . .

"I am of opinion that the statute of Louisiana is consistent with the personal liberty of citizens, white and black, in that State, and hostile to both the spirit and letter of the Constitution of the

United States. . . .

"For the reasons stated, I am constrained to withhold my assent for the opinion and judgment of the majority."

Immediately following the *Plessy v. Ferguson* decision, the U.S. Supreme Court declared literacy tests legal because the rules applied to both blacks and whites and were, therefore, nondiscriminatory.

Minorities in America, including women, did not have a lot to cheer about at the turn of the century. All the great strides that had been made during Reconstruction were reversing. It was like taking one step forward, then two steps backward.

Cameos

THADDEUS STEVENS

Thaddeus Stevens was born on April 4, 1792, in Danville, Vermont. He was graduated from Dartmouth College in 1814 and practiced law in Pennsylvania for fifteen years before being elected to Congress.

Stevens is best remembered for being one of the founders of the Republican party in 1855 in Pennsylvania. His work during Reconstruction earned him respect and rejection, both of which he knew how to handle. Stevens was a fiery speaker who rarely backed down in a good word fight. He died in August 1868.

CHARLES SUMNER

Charles Sumner was born in 1811 in Boston. He was graduated from Harvard Law School and then studied in Europe. He was admitted to the Massachusetts bar at the age of twenty-three. Sumner served in the United States Senate from 1851 until his death in 1874.

Sumner is best known for his strong support of civil rights legislation during Reconstruction and for being the author of the Civil Rights Act of 1875. Before the Civil War, Senator Sumner's antislavery position earned him the hatred of his southern colleagues.

Preston S. Brooks, a congressman from South Carolina, attacked Sumner on the floor of the Senate and struck Sumner until he was unconscious. It took the senator three years to regain his health. Even though he could not serve, he was reelected because Massachusetts's antislavery sympathizers believed that his vacant seat spoke volumes against the brutality of slaveholders.

Throughout his life, Sumner fought against racism, bigotry, and prejudice by pushing first for emancipation and then for civil rights legislation that protected all citizens from tyranny.

HIRAM REVELS

Hiram Revels was a United States senator from the state of Mississippi from February 25, 1870, to March 3, 1871. He was one of two black men to serve in the United States Senate during Reconstruction.

Senator Revels was born in Fayetteville, North Carolina, in 1822. At an early age he was sent to Ohio, where he was educated by the Quakers. During the first half of the nineteenth century, it was illegal to educate blacks in the South. Revels later was graduated from Knox College in Galesburg, Illinois.

Revels entered the ministry and served as pastor to several African Methodist Episcopal congregations in southern states. After the Civil War, Revels settled in Natchez, Mississippi, where he began his political career. First holding local and state offices, he earned his seat in Congress.

Later in life, Senator Revels became the president of Alcorn University near Lorman, Mississippi. He remained active in education and religion until his death in 1901.

ULYSSES S. GRANT

Ulysses S. Grant was born in 1822 in Point Pleasant, Ohio. He was graduated from West Point Military Academy and rose to become commander of the Union army during the Civil War. In 1868 and 1872 he was elected president of the United States, a job for which he was not suited.

During Grant's administration, Reconstruction flourished, but so did corruption, fraud, and scandal. Grant's major downfall was that he placed his trust in people who misused it.

After he served as president, Grant continued to be the victim of fraud. He became a partner in a banking house, but two of the partners mishandled the funds, and Grant was left penniless. *Century* magazine requested that he write his personal story, which he did. It was an honest account of his life, and it earned over a half a million dollars. But he died before he could enjoy it—or lose it.

Grant's famous tomb is located on Riverside Drive in New York City.

FREDERICK DOUGLASS

Frederick Douglass was born a slave in 1817, but he escaped to freedom in 1838. He worked for a while as a caulker but later joined the antislavery movement.

Douglass was an excellent speaker. His audiences were amazed at how well he spoke. It led some of his critics to wonder if he had ever been a slave. To prove that he had, Douglass wrote his autobiography, the *Life and Times of Frederick Douglass*, in which he chronicled his life from the eastern shores of Maryland to his escape and his life in freedom. That ended the rumors.

Douglass was an outspoken leader in the fight against slavery and later against racism and prejudice. During his life he was a newspaper publisher, writer, lecturer, adviser to presidents, husband, and father. He advocated the rights of women and fought against the ill treatment of other minorities in the United States.

Frederick Douglass had spent all his adult life fighting for freedom and justice in America for all people, men and women. It seemed fitting to many that this man should be honored with a presidential appointment. Amid controversy and criticism from blacks and whites, Douglass accepted President Hayes's appointment as marshal of the District of Columbia. Douglass went on to serve in other governmental posts, including minister and consul general to Haiti.

POSITIONS HELD BY FREDERICK DOUGLASS

Secretary of the Santo Domingo Commission	1871
Marshal of the District of Columbia	1877-1881
Recorder of Deeds for District of Columbia	1881-1886
U.S. Minister and Consul General to Haiti	1889-1891

A FEW NATIVE AMERICAN LEADERS

Geronimo—Apache

Victorio—Apache

Sitting Bull—Sioux

Chief Joseph—Nez Percé

Quanah Parker—Comanche

A memorial to Booker T. Washington by Augustus Saint Gaudens at Tuskegee Institute in Alabama

BOOKER T. WASHINGTON

Born a slave in 1856, Booker T. Washington rose to become a great American leader. His first love, however, was teaching.

When the Civil War ended, Washington knew that the only way to improve life was to get an education. He worked his way to Hampton, Virginia, where he settled and began studying for a teaching degree, which he received in 1875.

He accepted a teaching position at Hampton, where he successfully trained seventy-five American Indians. Washington did so well that he was made principal of the Negro Normal School in Tuskegee, Alabama, in 1881.

Seeing the school for the first time was disappointing. The building leaked, and he had no money for repairs. But he refused to give up.

From those humble beginnings, Tuskegee Institute began. Today it stands as a tribute to what hard work and effort can achieve. Booker T. Washington's autobiography, *Up from Slavery*, is still inspiring readers of all races, colors, and creeds.

| J. P. Morgan | John D. Rockefeller | Andrew Carnegie |

THE GREAT INDUSTRIALISTS

Between 1865 and 1900 great fortunes were made and lost. Three men rose to power during this period: John D. Rockefeller, Andrew Carnegie, and J. P. Morgan. These men were known as the "money men."

At one time, John D. Rockefeller controlled 90 percent of the country's oil empire. Andrew Carnegie, a Scottish immigrant, earned a fortune in the steamship, railroad, and steel industries. J. P. Morgan made his fortune in banking.

Once these men had acquired their wealth, they then spent the rest of their lives trying to give it away. Rockefeller, Carnegie, and Morgan were especially charitable, Morgan being a very generous contributor to black educational institutions. Their monetary gifts helped to build dormitories, libraries, hospitals, and laboratories in black schools all over the South.

THE STATUE OF LIBERTY

The Statue of Liberty is America's most recognizable landmark. It is hard to imagine going to New York and not finding her in the harbor. But before 1886 she was not there.

The statue was a gift from France and was designed by artist Frédéric Auguste Bartholdi. It was built in France and shipped here at a cost of $450,000.

Congress authorized the use of Bedloe's Island (about 2,950 yards from New York City) as a permanent home for her. Today it is called Liberty Island.

Americans conducted a fund-raising drive to help raise the $350,000 for the statue's pedestal. The Statue of Liberty is 305 feet, 6 inches high, and weighs 450,000 pounds. Another fund-raising drive was conducted to restore the statue for her one-hundredth birthday. The rededication of the statue was held on July 4, 1986. From the day she was unveiled on October 28, 1886, the Statue of Liberty has been *the* symbol of American freedom.

Booker T. Washington

W.E.B. DuBois

BOOKER T. AND W.E.B.

By Dudley Randall (1914-   )
From a collection titled *Poem Counterpoem*

"It seems to me," said Booker T.,
"It shows a mighty lot of cheek
To study chemistry and Greek
When Mister Charles needs a hand
To hoe the cotton on his land,
And when Miss Ann looks for a cook,
Why stick your nose inside a book?"

"I don't agree" said W.E.B.
"If I should have the drive to seek
Knowledge of chemistry or Greek,
I'll do it. Charles and Miss can look
Another place for hand and cook.
Some men rejoice in skill of hand,
And some in cultivating land.
But there are others who maintain
The right to cultivate the brain."

"It seems to me," said Booker T.,
"That all you folks have missed the boat
Who shout about the right to vote,
And spend vain days and sleepless nights
In uproar over civil rights.
Just keep your mouths shut, do not grouse,
But work, and save, and buy a house."

"I don't agree," said W.E.B.,
"For what can property avail
If dignity and justice fail?
Unless you help to make the laws,
They'll steal your house with trumped-up clause.
A rope's as tight, a fire as hot,
No matter how much cash you've got.
Speak soft, and try your little plan,
But as for me, I'll be a man."

"It seems to me," said Booker T.—

"I don't agree,"
said W.E.B.

SYMPATHY

By Paul Laurence Dunbar (1872-1906)
From *The Complete Poems of Paul Laurence Dunbar*
Dodd, Mead and Company, Inc., publisher

Dunbar is best remembered for his whimsical dialect poetry. But Dunbar's serious poetry is stirring and beautiful. Here is an example:

I know what the caged bird feels, alas!
   When the sun is bright on the upland slopes;
When the wind stirs soft through the springing grass,
And the river flows like a stream of glass;
   When the first bird sings and the first bud opes,
And the faint perfume from its chalice steals—
I know what the caged bird feels!

I know why the caged bird beats his wing
   Till its blood is red on the cruel bars;
For he must fly back to his perch and cling
When he fain would be on the bough a-swing;
   And a pain still throbs in the old, old scars
And they pulse again with a keener sting—
I know why he beats his wing!

I know why the caged bird sings, ah me,
   When his wing is bruised and his bosom sore,—
When he beats his bars and he would be free;
It is not a carol of joy or glee,
   But a prayer that he sends from his heart's deep core,
But a plea, that upward to Heaven he flings—
I know why the caged bird sings!

PRESIDENTS FROM 1865 TO 1900

Abraham Lincoln	1861-65	Chester A. Arthur	1881-85
Andrew Johnson	1865-69	Grover Cleveland	1885-89
Ulysses S. Grant	1869-77	Benjamin Harrison	1889-93
Rutherford B. Hayes	1877-81	Grover Cleveland	1893-97
James A. Garfield	1881	William McKinley	1897-1901

ABRAHAM LINCOLN

ANDREW JOHNSON

ULYSSES S. GRANT

RUTHERFORD B. HAYES

JAMES A. GARFIELD

CHESTER A. ARTHUR

GROVER CLEVELAND

BENJAMIN HARRISON

WILLIAM McKINLEY

ACCEPTANCE LETTER OF GENERAL ULYSSES S. GRANT, MAY 29, 1868

If Grant's letter of acceptance sets a record for brevity, it could also claim to have set the tone for the Republican campaign with its ringing phrase "Let Us Have Peace."

To Gen. Joseph R. Hawley, President National Republican Convention:

In formally accepting the nomination of the National Union Republican Convention of the 21st of May inst., it seems proper that some statement of views beyond the mere acceptance of the nomination should be expressed. The proceedings of the Convention were marked with wisdom, moderation and patriotism, and, I believe, express the feelings of the great mass of those who sustained the country through its recent trials. I indorse their resolutions. If elected to the office of President of the United States, it will be my endeavor to administer all the laws in good faith, with economy, and with the view of giving peace, quiet and protection everywhere. In times like the present it is impossible, or at least eminently improper, to lay down a policy to be adhered to, right or wrong, through an administration of four years. New political issues, not foreseen, are constantly arising, the views of the public on old ones are constantly changing, and a purely administrative officer should always be left free to execute the will of the people. I always have respected that will, and always shall. Peace, and universal prosperity—its sequence—with economy of administration, will lighten the burden of taxation, while it constantly reduces the national debt. Let us have peace.

With great respect, your obedient servant,

Many methods were used to trick the Indians out of their lands, including offering them liquor.

THE DAWES ACT

In 1887 Congress passed the Dawes Act, which encouraged American Indians individually to own land. The act gave to each head of an Indian family 160 acres of land and eighty acres to a single adult. Titles were withheld for fifteen years, during which time the Indians could not sell or lease the land.

Although a few families developed their land, the Dawes Act was not as successful as those who designed it had hoped. Indians were mainly nomads who did not believe in the independent ownership of land. In addition, the land they were given was the poorest farmland in the country. Later, when oil and other minerals were found on Indian lands, they became very valuable. Corrupt government officals, working with unprincipled businessmen, cheated Indians out of their land again.

In 1934, the Wheeler-Howard Act ended the land allotment and returned ownership to the various tribes.

THE BACK-TO-AFRICA MOVEMENT

Liberia is a West African country that was settled by former black Americans. The American Colonization Society, founded in 1817, helped to send eleven thousand former slaves back to Africa. The first settlement was at Cape Masurado in Liberia. Later the city was renamed Monrovia, after James Monroe, a supporter of the Colonization Society. Another well-known supporter was James Madison.

In 1847 Liberia became the Independent Republic of Liberia and had a government based on American democracy. Monrovia was made its capital. After the Civil War, some blacks returned to Africa, but not many.

A street in Monrovia, the capital of Liberia, from a drawing of the 1880s

Creek Indian schoolchildren

THE COMPULSORY INDIAN EDUCATION LAW

"Civilization" usually meant the assimilation of the Indian into the dominant white culture. After the Indian wars ended, an attempt was made to "civilize" Indians through education.

In 1817 Congress passed the Compulsory Indian Education Law. Boarding schools were established away from the reservations. Indian children were separated from their parents and culture and were taught the white man's dress, language, customs, and beliefs. By killing the "Indian" in the children, it was believed, they were being made suitable to live in society.

Boarding schools were established by missionaries at Fort Defiance in New Mexico, and in 1890 another was started in Grand Junction, Colorado. These two schools were to serve all the southwestern Indians. This was the dominant mode of education for Indian children until the 1930s.

A Brookings Institution study issued in 1928 revealed the terrible conditions that existed at these schools. The reports exposed "the outmoded teaching methods, primitive housing facilities for the students, staff cruelties toward the Indians, and the requirements that malnourished children work half a day in laundries, dairies, and shops." The policy of assimilation through separation was a failure.

In 1934 statistics further verified the Brookings report. Only eight thousand out of thirteen thousand Indian children attended school. It was not until the 1960s that education was shifted back to the reservation. But even in 1970, education among the Indians lagged behind the national norm.

WOUNDED KNEE

By 1886 all Native Americans had been defeated—the Apaches being the last. Geronimo was captured and sent to Fort Sill in Oklahoma, miles away from his native Southwest desert. Reservation life was almost unbearable—it was a slow death. There was not much reason to hope for anything better. It was the massacre at Wounded Knee, South Dakota, that summarized the fate of the American Indian.

On June 25, 1876, General George Custer, a glory-seeking presidential hopeful, led a 266-man company in what he thought was a surprise attack on the Sioux and other Plains Indians. Custer and his men were attacked by nearly twenty-five hundred Sioux Indians at the Little Bighorn River in Montana Territory. There was not one human survivor among the troops. (For years there was a myth that a black man had been spared. There is no proof that supports this story.)

A decade later the Sioux, like other tribes, were confined to reservations. Indians, accustomed to living a nomadic life, hated the confinement of the reservation. They sought freedom any way they could.

By 1890 an old combination of mysticism and cultural pride caused the rise of a militant movement among the various Indian bands. To join this new religious movement, participants had to learn the Ghost Dance. This ancient ritualistic dance was supposed to protect Indians from bullets and make the white man disappear.

At first, the authorities ignored the movement. But the group frightened reservation agents, who asked for help. The Seventh Cavalry, the outfit that had been hit so hard at the Little Bighorn, was sent in. Resentment toward the Sioux ran high, from officers to enlisted men. They were itching for an opportunity to vindicate themselves.

On the morning of December 29, 1890, they got their chance. Two Seventh Cavalry squadrons and a company of artillerymen tried to disarm a band of Indians that was led by Chief Big Foot at Wounded Knee Creek in South Dakota. Suddenly, someone began doing the Ghost Dance. A gun was fired. When the smoke cleared, about two hundred Indians had been killed. Their bodies were left until New Year's Day, when they were buried in a common grave. It was called the "Battle of Wounded Knee," but in reality it was a massacre in the legitimate use of the word.

For the most part, that incident ended the Indian wars. The land could be settled. Between 1876 and 1900, North and South Dakota, Montana, Washington, Idaho, Wyoming, and Utah were admitted into the United States. To the Native American these were meaningless and foolish boundaries, for "nobody owns the land!"

Part II

Separate as the Fingers on the Hand

TIME LINE 1901-1929

1901   Theodore Roosevelt becomes president after William McKinley's assassination

1904   Chinese immigration suspended indefinitely

1905   Niagara Movement

1906   Susan B. Anthony dies; the *Brownsville* case—127 members of the Twenty-fifth Infantry dishonorably discharged

1910   NAACP founded

1912   Immigration peaks; Woodrow Wilson elected president; federal employee facilities segregated

1915   Booker T. Washington dies

1918   World War I ends

1919   The rise of Marcus Garvey; Red Summer—blacks lynched by the hundreds; second Pan-African meeting in Paris; Three-hundredth year that blacks have been Americans

1920   Prohibition (Eighteenth Amendment); Women given right to vote (Nineteenth Amendment)

1921   Immigration numbers limited

1925   Marcus Garvey imprisoned

1929   Stock market crashes

Mary McLeod Bethune picketing for civil rights

_1901-1929_

SEGREGATION

Society was well ordered by the turn of the twentieth century. White men controlled the wealth and politics of the nation. Blacks, women, children, and immigrants had their "place," and that was where they were expected to stay.

America was mostly segregated in 1900. Segregation had become an acceptable social system that was instituted by various state laws and upheld by the Supreme Court. Although some states had integrated schools and public facilities, social mingling among the races or among economic classes was not acceptable even in the most liberal circles.

The South was rigidly segregated. Two communities existed side by side—one white, the other black—separate and very unequal. The laws that allowed segregation to work for so long were called "Jim Crow" laws.

Jim Crow

The term "Jim Crow" originated in the 1800 minstrel shows. White entertainers darkened their faces and performed skits that featured slaves. The most popular minstrel show character was a black crow named Jim. Jim Crow became a stereotyped

representation of black people and a name despised by slaves. After slavery was abolished, Jim Crow was associated with laws that restricted the rights of former slaves. By 1900 *Jim Crow* was a synonym for *segregation.*

DEMOCRACY AND SEGREGATION

The race issue was not a primary concern of politicians in the early 1900s. America was rapidly becoming a world power and a champion of democracy. Somehow, leaders were able to justify the existence of segregation in a democratic society by stressing the point that the races were separate but equal. This position would later become an embarrassment to American leaders who criticized other countries about their human rights policies.

Two presidents who helped shape the future of the nation in the early 1900s were men with both style and substance: Theodore Roosevelt (1901-1909) and Woodrow Wilson (1913-

The assassination of President McKinley

1921). Political and popular opinion, however, did not support their positions against segregation.

President Roosevelt

William McKinley was assassinated six months after he began his second term as president. Vice-President Theodore Roosevelt took the oath of office in September 1901.

Roosevelt was a robust, outspoken, energetic man, and a

personable president who was affectionately nicknamed "Teddy," or "TR." Roosevelt had a style that endeared him to ordinary people, and he used his popularity to bring about substantive reform in government, business, and industry. By exposing corruption and spotlighting wrongdoings, Roosevelt was able to muster public support for many of his progressive reforms. But Progressives split on the issues of woman suffrage and segregation. At the time, reformers did not include in their programs giving women the right to vote or granting blacks equal opportunity.

Personally, President Roosevelt was opposed to racial discrimination; for example, he spoke out against limitations set on Chinese immigration. Still Congress suspended Chinese immigration indefinitely in 1904. Although Booker T. Washington dined with Roosevelt in the White House, in the rest of the country blacks were still being lynched daily. From 1882 to 1928, 3,397 black men, women, and children were lynched in the United States. Very often their only crime was having been born the wrong color.

President Wilson

William H. Taft served one term after Roosevelt and was followed by Woodrow Wilson, a Democrat and a scholar. During his campaign, Wilson had said that he hoped "justice [could be] done to the colored people in every matter; and not mere grudging justice, but justice executed with liberality and cordial good feeling."

At first there was hope among blacks that Wilson was going to be true to his word. Once in office, however, President Wilson yielded to the political pressure prevalent at that time and issued

Booker T. Washington giving an address at Carnegie Hall in 1906 commemorating the twenty-fifth anniversary of the founding of Tuskegee University

an executive order that would segregate eating and restroom facilities among federal employees. Washington, D.C., the center of the free world, was a segregated city.

William Trotter, a black newspaper publisher, issued the strongest attack on Wilson's actions: "As equal citizens and by virtue of your public promises we are entitled at your hands to freedom from discrimination, restriction, imputation and insult in government employ. Have you a 'new freedom' for white Americans and a new slavery for your 'Afro-American fellow citizens'? God Forbid!"

Public opinion supported segregation. So for the time being, segregation and democracy coexisted. And strong leaders like Wilson and Roosevelt, who personally opposed the system, could not change it.

A FEW STEPS FORWARD . . .

Presidents Roosevelt, Taft, and Wilson have never been credited with being civil rights advocates. Yet during their administrations, children, women, and immigrants made a few steps forward in the long struggle for equal rights and justice.

Child Labor

Between 1901 and 1929, women had very few rights. Blacks had even fewer. And children had none. Child abuse ran rampant throughout the United States and occurred in all social, ethnic, and economic groups. Very few public or private agencies defended children's rights. Laws generally gave parents full authority over their children.

At that time, there were no age limitations on child labor. Children often worked to help support their families instead of attending school. Orphans and runaways worked to survive.

Because they worked cheaply, children were hired to work in factories, mines, and mills. Many were immigrant children, poor whites, Mexican-Americans, and blacks. The average child worker was nine to fourteen years old; the typical work day was twelve to fourteen hours for up to six days a week. Working conditions were unsanitary and dangerous. Children operated machinery that they were too small or too tired to handle, so accidents happened frequently. Children were maimed, blinded, or killed regularly. Orphans were known to work in mills all day and sleep on the floor underneath equipment at night.

During Theodore Roosevelt's administration, writers known as "muckrakers" exposed industries that used child labor. The country called for reform in this area.

Children were used to sort and break up coal after it had been mined. Some of them wear a covering over their noses to shield them from the coal dust.

It was not until May 25, 1908, under William Taft's administration, that Congress enacted a bill that regulated child labor in the District of Columbia. It was the hope of the Congress that states would follow their example. Some did, but the majority did not. Several southern states raised the age limit to fourteen for employment in mills and factories, but the law was disregarded, especially among sharecroppers and Appalachian miners.

On September 1, 1916, during President Wilson's administration, Congress enacted the Keating-Owen Act, which prohibited the interstate sale of any item made by children. It was a big step forward in the control of child labor.

On June 2, 1924, a child labor amendment was sent to the states for ratification. But the country, led by the South, did not pass it. The act failed. Union leaders, educators, pastors, judges, and other people worked to help pass state child-protection laws. But it was not until the 1930s that substantial child-labor laws were passed. Until that time, children remained unprotected by law, and so did women. But more and more women were becoming aware that, without the right to vote, they were powerless to change their situation.

Women Gain the Right to Vote

Susan B. Anthony died in 1906, never seeing her work for woman suffrage completed. Carrie Chapman Catt, a very capable woman, took up the battle where Anthony left off. The woman suffrage movement gained momentum starting in 1906 during the Roosevelt administration and it climaxed in 1920 with the passage of the Nineteenth Amendment. Women were determined to get the right to vote, and a growing number of men agreed with them, even though it was not popular to admit it.

Dr. Anna Shaw and Mrs. Carrie Chapman Catt lead twenty thousand women in a march for suffrage down Fifth Avenue in New York City in 1918.

Sojourner Truth

Historically, the American woman suffrage movement began in 1848 when a group of women met in Seneca Falls, New York, to set forth their demands for civil rights. Lucretia Mott and Elizabeth Cady Stanton helped organize the meeting and emerged as leaders. Sojourner Truth, a black woman, was also an outspoken supporter of abolition and woman suffrage. Her famous "Ain't I a Woman" speech became a suffrage classic. However, at the time that Sojourner Truth delivered the speech, a few women objected to associating with blacks for fear that it might diminish their efforts. Susan B. Anthony led the movement in the latter half of the nineteenth century.

In 1848, women could not own property, sign contracts, sue, serve on juries, or vote. The only rights they had were those given to them by their fathers, brothers, and husbands. At the beginning of the twentieth century, women were not in any better shape.

Women were still considered too delicate and fragile to handle business matters. Described as "the weaker sex," women were subject to "nervous collapse and fits of emotional outbursts." Women needed supervision in matters regarding money and property. In literature, drama, art, and music, women were stereotyped as all-loving and all-forgiving or as devious, possessive, cunning, and vindictive. Young girls had very few role models in business, medicine, law, and politics. In fact, a career-minded woman was a "vexation to her father"!

A lot of women did as much as men did to perpetuate female myths. Antisuffrage associations were formed to "save motherhood and the family." A large number of women believed that voting was vulgar and degrading. Still, Carrie Catt carried the struggle forward. She was a bright, enthusiastic college graduate who managed to get union support for the movement. Labor proved to be an excellent ally.

Women put pressure on state officials, and, between 1910 and 1913, more states granted women the right to vote. But progress was slow, and women grew impatient. A more brilliant suffrage group, headed by Alice Paul and Lucy Burns, was formed. They picketed and held mass marches and rallies. Very often during a suffrage rally women were shoved and kicked by other women.

When a large group of women picketed the White House during World War I, they were pelted with tomatoes and eggs, then arrested. Several women were injured during the arrest. When the suffragists staged a hunger strike in jail, they were force-fed by having tubes shoved down their throats.

President Woodrow Wilson intervened on the suffragists'
behalf, perhaps influenced by his wife and by his daughter, who
was a suffragist. Afterward, the president personally asked
Congress to pass the bill that proposed women's voting rights and
that had been introduced by S. S. Sergant in 1886. In a dramatic
gesture, Representative Harry Blanchard was carried in on a
stretcher to cast the deciding two-thirds vote in the House. The
amendment passed the House but was defeated in the Senate.
Hopes were crushed. Then on June 4, 1919, the Senate took
another vote. This time it passed. The Nineteenth Amendment
was ratified by thirty-five states in record time, and on August 26,
1920, it was signed into law.

*Lucy Burns was
jailed for her
activities as a
suffragette.*

Above: The National Women's party celebrating the passage of the Nineteenth Amendment. Alice Paul is on the balcony.
Left: Carrie Chapman Catt (left) and Mary Garrett Hay (right) casting their first vote in a presidential election.

The law did not revolutionize American politics. Women did not abandon the home, nor did they rush out to run for political offices. For the most part, women who exercised their right to vote did so the way that their fathers or husbands did. The fear that women would become a powerful political force just did not materialize, partly because women lost interest in the movement. The struggle against sex discrimination in employment and education would be fought by their granddaughters. Contrary to what people thought at the time, the women's movement was not over — it was just beginning.

The Huddled Masses: The Great Migration

Three-quarters of the American people are descendants of immigrants who came to the United States between 1840 and 1920. The period between 1900 and 1920, known as the Great Migration, peaked just before World War I.

Old men, children, young girls, grandmothers, students, servants, and whole families came to the United States. Sometimes all they owned was wrapped in a blanket or carried in a wicker basket. Thousands entered through Ellis Island, a twenty-nine-acre island in New York Harbor where facilities had been established to screen all incoming immigrants.

Other immigrants entered the United States through southern and western harbors. All convicts, idiots, lunatics, persons with diseases, polygamists, and political radicals were rejected — if they were discovered. Anyone with a physical handicap, who might not be able to work, and children under age sixteen without parents were returned to their native country.

During the Great Migration there were no restrictions placed on the number of immigrants who could enter the United States.

Slavic immigrants on Ellis Island in the early 1900s

There were no limitations placed on the number of immigrants allowed to enter from any country, except countries in Asia. By 1929 massive immigration to the United States had stopped. But American food, clothing, architecture, crafts, language, ideas, and customs were changed forever.

President Franklin D. Roosevelt said that America was like a patchwork of many cultures. Sewn together, Americans made one wonderfully colorful quilt. But Roosevelt also called for immigrants to assimilate. He wanted no more hyphenated Americans. He said, "We have room for but one language here, and that is the English language, for we intend to see that the crucible turns our people out as Americans." And many immigrants did what Roosevelt asked for.

Immigrants who quickly became Americanized—who learned American customs, ate American foods, wore American clothing, and spoke the American language—were accepted sooner. Those who would not abandon their religion or their rich cultural heritage were locked out of the American mainstream. Jews, Orientals, Hispanics, and some Italians, for example, were never

John L. Lewis (left) and Samuel Gompers (right) were organizers in the labor movement.

able to "blend in." They experienced discrimination longer than did other immigrant groups.

Each ethnic group went through a period when its people were discriminated against. Ironically, when an ethnic group rose to power, they very often were guilty of discrimination against others. For example, Samuel Gompers, an English immigrant who founded the American Federation of Labor (AFL), denounced all Asian workers, which included Japanese, Chinese, and South Pacific islanders. He refused them union membership even in segregated locals. On the northwest Pacific Coast, Japanese were seen as rivals to white American laborers, and those who hired Japanese were often harassed by angry mobs of workers.

Most of the newcomers began by working as common laborers or domestic workers. They lived in deplorable tenement buildings where disease and fires were the major causes of death. They endured extreme poverty, ethnic stereotyping, and racial bigotry. It was not uncommon for employers to advertise, "Wanted: Good

Christian Workers." That, of course, excluded Jews and other non-Christians. Being Catholic was not acceptable either. Catholics were discriminated against, especially in the South, where they were victims of Klan terror. All kinds of unfair hiring and housing practices were used in the early 1900s to keep out "undesirable" groups.

However, as the white immigrants became citizens, they were automatically given full rights of citizenship—the right to vote, hold office, serve on juries, own property, borrow money, and begin businesses. Using the opportunities available to them in education and business, they lifted themselves out of poverty and degradation. Rising out of poverty was not so easy for black Americans.

At the end of the nineteenth century, immigrants lived in squalid conditions.
This man's home was a coal cellar.

THE STRUGGLE FOR IDENTITY

Blacks were angered when newly-arrived white immigrants became citizens and were granted full citizenship. Blacks resented being lorded over by people whose citizenship papers were not quite dry.

In a vain attempt to assimilate, too many blacks decided to try what the immigrants had done. They cast aside their heritage and embraced all that was acceptable by white standards. It proved to be a costly mistake. All things associated with "blackness" were discarded. An alarming number of black women measured their beauty by white standards. They were made to feel ashamed of their dark skin, high cheekbones, full lips, and kinky hair. Fortunes were made by people who created creams and lotions that promised to lighten dark skin and straighten hair. Even the term "black" was considered a gross insult, almost as offensive as "nigger." "Colored" and "Negro" were thought to be far more acceptable terms.

In far too many instances, blacks showed no interest in their African heritage. Slavery was not discussed. And the natural love of color, music, and dance was suppressed.

Booker T. Washington had encouraged black people to become "more like whites in dress and manner." But for all their efforts, it did not change a thing. A well-educated female black teacher could not vote in Mississippi because she was a woman and was black.

Even within a segregated society where opportunities were limited, blacks managed to make outstanding achievements. Education was revered, so more and more young men and women took advantage of whatever educational opportunities were

Dr. George Washington Carver in his laboratory at Tuskegee Institute

available. In 1901 thirty thousand blacks were educators, and 1.5 million were enrolled in school.

George Washington Carver earned international acclaim as a chemist, among many other achievements. He discovered countless uses for the peanut, such as peanut butter spread, peanut oil, and others. Dr. Daniel Hale Williams performed what is believed to be the first open-heart surgery in America. Matthew

Dr. Daniel Hale Williams (left), performed what is believed to be the first open-heart surgery in America. Matthew Henson (right) was Admiral Peary's assistant in the expedition that discovered the North Pole.

Henson was with Admiral Peary when they discovered the North Pole. And in 1908 the community sent up a collective cheer when Jack Johnson became the first black heavyweight boxing champion.

Carter Woodson, Historian

Since blacks and whites did not socialize together, they did not know much about each other. Numerous myths and stereotypes were created out of ignorance. Many textbooks that were in use at the time contained inaccurate information that supported common ethnic stereotypes. History books did not include the contributions of black people and other minorities, so children grew up believing that black people had made no contribution to the growth and development of America. Schoolchildren, and very often their teachers, had never heard of Frederick Douglass,

Jack Johnson was the first black to win the heavyweight title. He was inducted into the Boxing Hall of Fame in 1954.

Nat Turner, Harriet Tubman, Sojourner Truth, and other great Americans who had lived less than fifty years earlier.

For these reasons the works of Carter Woodson are important. Woodson was considered a militant at the time, but he did a great deal to preserve black history and to record it accurately. Angered by white historians and writers who were guilty of distributing unscientific information about black people, and frustrated by black people's lack of knowledge about themselves, Carter Woodson set out to correct both situations. It was an overwhelming job, but he wrote several volumes of black history. He also organized the Association for the Study of Negro Life and History in 1915. This organization was designed to help black people overcome their own negative feelings about themselves. In 1926 Woodson introduced Negro History Week, which is celebrated in February of each year.

THE RISE OF BLACK MILITANCY

The gulf between Booker T. Washington and W.E.B. DuBois grew wider and wider. In the winter of 1904, Washington called fifty black leaders to a meeting at Carnegie Hall in New York City. (Travel arrangements were paid by Andrew Carnegie.) DuBois agreed to attend. At the meeting Washington proposed that a "Committee of Twelve" be founded to advance the interest of blacks. The proposal was carried out. But Washington packed the committee with his followers, placing the organization under his control. When DuBois complained, it made him appear to be a spoiler, but he refused to back down, flatly rejecting the offer to be a token part of the group.

The Niagara Movement

In June 1905 DuBois sent a letter to black intellectuals. It read, in part,

> The time seems more than ripe for organization, determined and aggressive action on the part of men who believe in Negro freedom and growth. Movements are on foot threatening individual freedom and our self-respect. I write you to propose a conference during the coming summer.

Hotels on the New York side of Niagara Falls refused DuBois a place to hold the meeting; he crossed over to the Canadian side, where Ontario hotels were more hospitable. Twenty-nine young blacks from fourteen states answered DuBois's call. The power of the falls seemed to symbolize their goal to gain full rights of manhood. So they named the group the Niagara Movement. They left there committed to the struggle for black equality. "And we want it now, henceforth and forever," they said.

The group that formed the Niagara Movement

The movement quickly attracted young college students. The following year, the meeting was held in Virginia, where John Brown, the militant abolitionist, had led an unsuccessful assault on the arsenal at Harper's Ferry.

The organization had leadership and commitment but no money. It could not continue.

The National Association for the Advancement of Colored People (NAACP)

An antiblack race riot erupted during the summer of 1908 in Springfield, Ohio. William Walling, a noted writer, called for "a revival of the abolitionists' spirit." Mary White Ovington, Oswald Willard, and Dr. Henry Moskowitz joined Walling. Using February 12, 1909—the one-hundredth birthday of Abraham Lincoln—as a rallying point, this group of whites met to discuss how they might help.

Out of that meeting came a document that called for blacks and whites to work actively toward obtaining legal rights for black Americans. The "call" was signed by pastors, social workers, novelists, and educators, both male and female. Many of these people were second-generation immigrants whose parents had suffered the injustices of discrimination because of their religion and national origin.

Five blacks, including W.E.B. DuBois, also signed the document, which later became the foundation on which the National Association for the Advancement of Colored People (NAACP) was incorporated in 1910. The NAACP was the opposing force against racist organizations such as the Ku Klux Klan. The Klan used violence to force their will on society. The NAACP chose to fight in the courtrooms, to wage war on unjust laws and discriminatory legislation. At last, DuBois had the support that he needed to further his ideas. He was asked to be the director of research and the first editor of *Crisis*, the official publication of the NAACP. There were board members who were concerned about DuBois's scathing attacks on Booker T. Washington. DuBois insisted that, if he were to be the editor of the *Crisis*, he had to have full control over its editorial position. Although the relationship between DuBois and the board of directors was stormy in the early years, the problems were settled by 1918. DuBois had to give a little—something he found difficult to do— and so did the directors. White people, even those who were liberal, were not accustomed to dealing with forceful black men.

The flaming cross of the Ku Klux Klan lights up the night.

In the same year the National Urban League was formed by white social workers. Their purpose was to help rural blacks adjust to urban life, which included aid in housing, job training, education, and employment.

William Monroe Trotter, Militant Leader

There were some leaders who believed that blacks should be responsible for forming their own organizations without help from whites. This idea was considered militant in the early 1900s. One spokesman for that position was William Monroe Trotter. Trotter, an honor graduate from Harvard University, was a leading militant of the day. He wanted blacks to control their own organizations, and he criticized DuBois for working with the interracial NAACP.

DuBois, also labeled a militant, may have agreed with his friend Trotter in theory, but DuBois was not convinced that the militant approach would get the fastest or the best results. DuBois reminded Trotter that the lack of funding was often the demise of black organizations. In fact it had not been the lack of commitment that had caused the Niagara Movement to fail—it was the lack of money. DuBois pointed out that money from millionaire philanthropists had made Booker T. Washington a powerful leader. For the moment, the NAACP had given DuBois a platform for his ideas—he controlled the editorial policies of *Crisis* and was not about to give that up. But Trotter was equally convinced that white people working within a black organization would tend to control it, especially if they were funding the organization.

Trotter came from a wealthy black Boston family. Money was not a problem for him. With his inheritance he started his own newspaper, *The Guardian*, which reflected his views of the various issues that affected black Americans. In response to the NAACP, Trotter formed the National American Political League. He was, as DuBois admitted later, offering black people a choice in leadership.

THE BLACK SOLDIER FIGHTS TO PRESERVE DEMOCRACY

Booker T. Washington could not have described it better when he said that blacks and whites were "as separate as the fingers on the hand." But in times of war they were "one like the fist." Maybe one in aims, but the United States military was segregated even in times of war.

A drawing of the Spanish-American War by Fletcher C. Ransom is entitled: Forgotten Heroes—Troop C, 9th U.S. Cavalry, Capt. Taylor, leading the charge of San Juan Hill, Cuba.

The Spanish-American War

On February 15, 1898, in Havana Harbor, Cuba, the Spanish blew up the USS *Maine.* Twenty-two black men were among the casualties. Congress declared war, and hundreds of young men rushed to join the military.

Back home, reports of the all-black fighting units filled black communities with pride. The Ninth and the Tenth Cavalries were distinguished in the Battle of San Juan Hill. Colonel Theodore

Roosevelt's famous regiment, the Rough Riders, would not have survived if black soldiers had not come to their rescue.

The Spanish were defeated. Black and white men, fighting for a common cause, had won. Still, though, they fought in separate units. The black fighting units went on to serve in the Philippines, where they fought against a Filipino insurrection.

Not since Lincoln had a president spoken so highly of the black soldier. Theodore Roosevelt was greatly admired because of the honors he had bestowed on black soldiers collectively and individually. That is why everyone was deeply saddened by the *Brownsville* case.

The *Brownsville* Case

A black man with a gun was more frightening than anything else a racist could imagine. Nothing reflects this more than does the *Brownsville* case.

After serving in Cuba and the Philippines, the Twenty-fifth Infantry was sent to Fort Brown, in Brownsville, Texas. Most white citizens resented black soldiers and insulted them whenever they came to town. Naturally, there was anger on the part of men who had defended these people who were putting up signs stating, ''No niggers and no dogs allowed.''

On August 13, 1906, sixteen to twenty unidentified men rode through Brownsville, shooting at random. One man was killed, and several others were wounded. The townspeople insisted that soldiers from the Twenty-fifth Cavalry were responsible, but there were no witnesses.

During inspection the next morning, the battalion rifles were found to be clean and all ammunition accounted for. Later that day, the Brownsville Citizens' Committee, without any concrete evidence, concluded that the shots had been fired by soldiers. The soldiers were found guilty without benefit of a trial.

On August 29, 1906, the military submitted a hasty report that supported the citizens. All soldiers repeatedly denied knowing anything about the incident and presented proof of their whereabouts. Army investigators, however, called it a "conspiracy of silence" and issued a warning: "[The] black soldiers are much more aggressive . . . on the social equality question." After a military trial, the soldiers were declared guilty, even though the evidence was not conclusive.

President Roosevelt ordered an additional investigation. Then on November 26, 1906, 167 black soldiers of the Twenty-fifth Cavalry were dishonorably discharged from the United States Army. One man had served twenty-seven years in the army; twenty-five had served more than ten years, six were Medal of Honor winners, and thirteen had citations for bravery in the Spanish-American War.

These men were declared ineligible for pension and were denied the right to rejoin the army or the right to work for the government. Civil rights organizations continued to fight on their behalf, and within a year fourteen of the 167 were declared eligible for reenlistment—the records do not state why. Eleven of the fourteen reenlisted and received back pay.

On September 28, 1972, the army finally cleared the records of the 167 black soldiers who had been discharged for the shooting incident in Brownsville and declared that the original action was a gross injustice. The discharges were changed to "honorable." Dorsey Willis, then eighty-six, was the sole survivor of the original 167. In late 1973 Congress passed a bill that granted him $25,000 in compensation and provided him with medical care at a veterans hospital in Minneapolis until his death.

World War I

In 1914 there was talk of war again, in Europe. President Wilson promised Americans that the U.S. military forces would not be involved.

Repeated efforts were made to bar blacks from military service. These efforts were based on fears that armed black soldiers might lead an insurrection, although there was no evidence in military records to support such an idea. A bill was passed that would prohibit blacks from serving as commissioned and noncommissioned officers in the army and navy in 1914, but it never came to a vote. Then two years later Congress passed the National Defense Act, but no additional black units were opened. Southern congressmen sponsored a bill that would eliminate black soldiers and sailors from the armed forces by preventing enlistment or reenlistment of "any person of the Negro or Colored Race." (That included Orientals, Hispanics, Native Americans, and blacks.) Newton Baker, secretary of war, spoke out strongly against the bill, and the measure was defeated.

Then the inevitable happened. The United States entered World War I. DuBois encouraged blacks to participate willingly, telling them to "close ranks. Let us while this war lasts, forget our special grievances and close our ranks . . . with our white citizens." Four hundred thousand black men and women served in the military, and two hundred thousand served in Europe but in segregated units.

This is what General John J. Pershing, the commander in chief of the American Expeditionary Force, had to say about black soldiers:

Tribute to the Negro Soldier

The stories, probably invented by German agents, that colored soldiers

*General John J.
Pershing*

in France are always placed in most dangerous positions and sacrificed to save white soldiers, that when wounded they are left on the ground to die without medical attention, etc. are absolutely false.

A tour of inspection among American Negro troops by officers of these headquarters shows the comparatively high degree of training and efficiency among these troops. Their training is identical with that of other American troops serving with the French Army, the effort being to lead all American troops gradually to heavy combat duty by a preliminary service in trenches in quiet sectors.

Colored troops in trenches have been particularly fortunate as one regiment had been there a month before any losses were suffered. This was almost unheard of on the western front.

The exploits of two colored infantrymen in repelling a much larger German patrol, killing and wounding several Germans and winning the Croix de Guerre by their gallantry, has aroused a fine spirit of emulation throughout the colored troops, all of whom are looking forward to more active service.

The only regret expressed by colored troops is that they are not given more dangerous work to do. I cannot commend too highly the spirit shown among the colored combat troops, who exhibit fine capacity for quick training and eagerness for the most dangerous work.

Awards and medals did not change attitudes. In the midst of the war that was being fought to preserve democratic rights, there was a battle for human rights going on within the United States.

On August 23, 1917, a black soldier in Houston, Texas, asked a white police officer to stop beating a black woman. The officer turned on the soldier, beat him, and arrested him. One hundred black soldiers seized rifles and ammunition and went into Houston. When the cease-fire was called, sixteen white civilians and four black soldiers had been killed.

The next day the entire battalion was transferred to New Mexico. Sixty-four black soldiers were court-martialed for "murder and mutiny." Thirteen were sentenced to death and hanged, but not one white person served one day or was convicted of any crime.

Red Summer

Armistice Day, November 11, 1918, was when the war to end all wars was over. In New York City, on February 17, 1919, the famous 369th Infantry marched down Fifth Avenue to Harlem through cheering crowds. But 1919 was a pivotal year for black people in America.

Black soldiers were met with open hostility when they returned home. There were so many lynchings in the South that the poet James Weldon Johnson called it the Red Summer.

Chicago burst into flames, and riots followed in cities across the North. White mobs attacked black communities, and, suprisingly, blacks were arming themselves and fighting back. Race relations were strained to the breaking point.

Under the leadership of W.E.B. DuBois, blacks paused to recognize the tricentennial—three hundred years since Afro-Americans had first landed on this continent. He wrote in the *Crisis:*

A wounded World War I veteran of the Thirty-sixth Colored Infantry talks to spectators watching a parade in March 1919.

In sackcloth and ashes . . . we commemorate this [year], lest we forget; lest a single drop of blood, a single moan of pain, a single bead of sweat, in all these three, long, endless centuries should drop into oblivion.

Why must we remember? Is this by a counsel of Vengeance and Hate? God forbid! We must remember because if once the world forgets evil, evil is reborn; because if the suffering of the American Negro is once forgotten, then there is no [guarantee], down to the last pulse of time that Devils will not again enslave and murder and oppress the weak and unfortunate.

PAN-AFRICANISM

A group of middle-class American blacks, the most notable being W.E.B. DuBois, were present when the first formal Pan-African Congress was convened in London in 1900. Only a few representatives from African countries came. But the Congress provided a critical union between African countries and black Americans.

The second Pan-African Conference was organized by DuBois and held in Paris in 1919. The goal was to seek a firm connection "between the struggle for black freedom in America and the revolutionary movements of Africans in the homeland and elsewhere."

DuBois continued the exchange of information about the past and present, hoping for a more enlightened future for both people with a common history. At the same time, there was another movement under way that involved the uniting of Africans and Afro-Americans.

MARCUS GARVEY

Historians are still trying to find the appropriate slot into which they can place Marcus Garvey and the movement he represented. He has stubbornly refused to be categorized. For a while it was easy to dismiss him as a flamboyant buffoon. But Garvey would not conform to a definition. He never explained or apologized for his actions, so none will be offered here.

Marcus Garvey came along when poor black people needed what he was able to provide—a different kind of leadership. Booker T. Washington had died in 1915. For the most part, DuBois and Trotter represented middle-class, well-educated blacks. The masses of inner-city slum dwellers could not relate to them.

Marcus Garvey, organizer of the Universal Improvement Association, takes part in a parade.

Marcus Garvey was a bold and brassy leader. He appealed to the ordinary black man. He did not condemn the poor black masses for who and what they were. In fact, he told them that they were beautiful, and they believed him.

Garvey was a Jamaican who started the Universal Improvement Association. In 1919 he moved his headquarters to Harlem. The main thrust of his movement was for black people to emigrate to Africa, to help their brothers free themselves from European colonial powers and to begin a new republic. Such ideas made for inspirational speeches, but they made some people very uncomfortable.

DuBois was an advocate of African and Afro-American unity. But he attacked Garvey's approach, calling it lunacy. Garvey counterattacked, accusing DuBois of being a puppet of white so-called liberals. William Trotter was not spared either—Garvey labeled him an intellectual snob.

Garvey's followers grew to tens of thousands at a startling rate. The movement was not all talk and no action. Garvey encouraged black people to do for themselves and to stop waiting for whites to "give them the scraps from their plates."

Garvey was a segregationist who urged his people to take pride in their African heritage and to reject the trappings of a white racist society. He organized self-help programs in Harlem and other metropolitan cities. Garveyites sponsored day-care centers, youth centers, and business enterprises that hired blacks only.

But the ultimate question came: When was the mass exodus to Africa supposed to take place? Nobody, not even his closest aides, knew the date. In truth, Garvey did not know himself. By 1925 he was in prison, then later was exiled. He died alone and penniless in Europe.

The reasons for the demise of Garvey's movement are myriad. One was the black people's reluctance to leave America. Every back-to-Africa movement had essentially failed because black people refused to leave. For all its racial hatred, America was home. And, although neither race would have admitted it at the time, blacks and whites had more in common historically than blacks had in common with Africans or than whites had in common with Europeans. Truly, that was a dangerous realization. As quickly as it rose, the Garvey movement collapsed, or so it appeared.

The self-pride and self-determination that Garvey taught had made a difference to more than just a few. The marches and

The saxophone section of a band at the Cotton Club

speeches had ended for a time, but not the ideas. One day in the future those ideas would explode into another movement that had at its core the seeds of Garvey's philosophy.

THE HARLEM RENAISSANCE

The 1920s roared in on the heels of Prohibition. The Eighteenth Amendment was passed, making America a "dry" country— no liquor was to be made or sold legally within its borders. That did not stop many people from making it, buying it, selling it, or drinking it. For these people, the party never stopped. "Bathtub gin" and "moonshine" were made by the barrels and sold by the jar in back alleys and in swanky "speakeasies."

The 1920s provided an opportunity for black performers to showcase their talents before all-white audiences in places like the world-renowned Cotton Club. The Cotton Club was located in Harlem. The club was owned by whites, but all the performers were black. The patrons were white; no black customers were allowed to enter. It was typical of the times.

The radio and movie industries also offered America a modern form of entertainment. These two industries discriminated against blacks by denying them air time or by portraying them in stereotyped and degrading roles. Probably the most damaging stereotyping had been done in the 1915 film *Birth of a Nation.* Although it has been hailed as a technical masterpiece, its subject matter was used to justify brutal repression of black people.

Black artists flocked to Harlem in the 1920s. There they worked among their people and tried to represent their race accurately in all art forms. Poets, artists, musicians, and performers stunned and dazzled white audiences with their work. It was bold and dramatic, yet sensitively hopeful. They took the pain and suffering of a whole race and turned it into art. Out of this period, which is known as the Harlem Renaissance, great American artists developed. Langston Hughes was one of them.

Hughes sums up the literary themes of that period in this poem:

> I, too, sing America.
> I am the darker brother.
> They send me to eat in the kitchen
> When company comes,
> But I laugh,
> And eat well,
> And grow strong.
>
> Tomorrow,
> I'll be at the table
> When company comes.
> Nobody'll dare
> Say to me,
> "Eat in the kitchen,"
> Then.
>
> Besides,
> They'll see how beautiful I am
> And be ashamed—
>
> I, too, am America.

Langston Hughes (left) worked as a busboy when he was a young man. President Franklin Delano Roosevelt (right) preparing to make a radio broadcast

The Roaring Twenties came to a roaring halt in 1929. The stock market crashed, and the bottom fell out of the American economy. The United States was on the verge of economic disaster. The country needed someone to take control, to stop the descent into oblivion. In 1932 the nation elected as their president Franklin Delano Roosevelt.

Eleanor Roosevelt hands out gifts at the annual Christmas party at the Wiltwyck School for Boys in New York City.

TIME LINE 1930-1954

1930   The Depression worsens and unemployment grows

1932   Franklin D. Roosevelt elected president

1933   Roosevelt begins economic recovery program called the New Deal; First woman cabinet member, Frances Perkins, appointed secretary of labor; Prohibition repealed

1933-35   New Deal programs put into work: National Recovery Administration (NRA); Civilian Conservation Corps (CCC); Agricultural Adjustment Administration (AAA); Works Progress Administration (WPA); and National Youth Administration (NYA)

1934   Arthur Mitchell first black since Reconstruction to be elected to House of Representatives

1935   Black and white farmers form the Southern Tenant Farmers Union; Harlem riots

1936   Roosevelt reelected for second term; Adolf Hitler refuses to shake Jesse Owens's hand because he is black; rise of Nazism in Europe; oppression of Jews

1939   Europe in war

1941   Executive Order No. 8802 given, calling for fair employment practices in federal government; Pearl Harbor bombed by Japan on December 7

1942   Japanese-American internment

1943   Japanese-Americans allowed to join U.S. military but are confined to segregated units

1945   Roosevelt dies on April 12; Harry Truman becomes president; World War II ends on August 14

1948   Civil Rights Commission established

1950   Korean War begins

1952   General Dwight Eisenhower elected president; McCarthyism peaks

1954   *Brown v. Topeka* Supreme Court decision

A junkman collecting old paper during the Depression

1930-1954

ROOSEVELT'S NEW DEAL

Three million blacks and fifteen million whites were unemployed when Franklin Roosevelt took office in 1933. In his first inaugural speech, Roosevelt asked the American people for their support.

"In every dark hour of our national life a leadership of frankness and vigor has met with that understanding and support of people themselves which is essential to victory. I am convinced that you will again give that support to leadership in these critical days."

Then he rolled up his sleeves and went to work. Roosevelt had a plan, which came to be known as the New Deal. It created programs "of relief, recovery, and reforms." Black people were delighted to learn that they too were included in the New Deal.

Roosevelt followed through on his promises. During his administration fifty thousand black farmers received government loans, and the average income of blacks doubled. Still, two million black people were hungry, homeless, and poorer than ever.

In his second term, President Roosevelt pointed out that "one-third of a nation is ill-housed, ill-clad, and ill-nourished."

The blacks and the Indians felt that President Roosevelt was working to help them.

Part of Roosevelt's popularity grew out of a trust that the American people had for him. He kept them informed about the country's progress during his weekly "fireside chats," which were aired on radio. For the first time, citizens of all races, colors, and religions—rich and poor, male and female—felt a part of the government. The people called Roosevelt "our president" because he represented the "ordinary" person and not big business and industry. When the president asked Americans to work together to build on the hopes and dreams that had maintained America in other periods of crisis, they did.

President Roosevelt's enthusiasm spread, and people began to hope again. White families who had lost their homes, farms, and small businesses were able to borrow money to start over again. Hungry people were fed; housing was built for the homeless and hospitals and health centers were established for the sick, the disabled, and the aged.

In 1933 the National Recovery Administration (NRA) and the Civilian Conservation Corps (CCC) were started. The NRA created a set of five hundred codes that regulated businesses and industry. Competition was monitored, production limited, prices set, a minimum wage established, and child labor abolished. The CCC put employable young men back to work in the national parks and waterways. Prohibition also was repealed in 1933, which legalized hundreds of jobs that were associated with the liquor industry.

Interestingly enough, ten thousand black and white tenant farmers (many of the whites were Ku Klux Klan members) formed the Southern Tenant Farmers Union in 1935. They appealed to the government for help.

The New Deal continued with the Works Progress Administration (WPA), which was formed to put people back to work. The National Youth Administration (NYA) was added to the program and provided training for unemployed youths. Mary McLeod Bethune, a former college president, was placed in charge of black youth programs. Over two hundred thousand young black college students were employed in conservation and reclamation projects.

Secretary of Labor Frances Perkins inspects a naval gun factory in 1936.

In addition, Roosevelt appointed a woman, Frances Perkins, to his cabinet as secretary of labor, and among his closest aides were a multiracial group of men and women.

A FEW MORE STEPS FORWARD . . .

Although the black population had more than tripled since Reconstruction (4 million to 14.8 million), blacks were not proportionately represented in government. As northern states granted blacks the right to vote, that situation began to change, but slowly.

*Representative
Arthur W. Mitchell*

In 1934 Arthur W. Mitchell was elected to the House of
Representatives from the First Congressional District in Illinois.
From 1935 to 1945 he was the only black man in Congress and
was very active in the Roosevelt administration. It was a small
step forward.

In the 1930s Chicago and St. Louis citizens boycotted white-
owned businesses that were in the black communities but that had
no black employees. The boycotts were effective, and hiring
practices were made fairer—another step forward.

During the latter half of the 1930s, the Congress of Industrial
Organizations (CIO) was established. It was the first labor union
to include blacks, and by 1940 black membership numbered two
hundred thousand—one more step forward.

The Supreme Court ruled that the University of Missouri had to
admit a black to its law school because there were no black law
schools available in the state. According to the justices, the state's
"failure to provide an equal education . . . within the borders of
the state violated the U.S. Constitution"—that was a big step
forward.

It was in this way that black people chipped away at segregation and discrimination. It was a long, slow process that was discouraging at times. In fact, some people got tired of waiting for people to do right.

In New York, Harlem exploded into one of the worst riots in history in 1935. Centuries of rage were unleashed, and nothing could stop the outpouring of pent-up emotions and fury.

THE RISE OF NAZISM

At the 1936 Olympic Games in Munich, Germany, Jesse Owens made America proud by winning three gold medals. Adolf Hitler, leader of the German Nazi party, refused to shake the gold medalist's hand. Hitler believed that Germans were the superior race and were destined to rule the world and rule over others. Since Owens was black he was considered inferior by the führer. But Jesse Owens handled the insult with poise and grace. He was not too surprised; there were plenty of his countrymen who would not shake his hand either.

Even though Hitler's racism included blacks, it was concentrated on Jews, a people he had targeted for extinction. Throughout the centuries, Jews had been the victims of several European purges. So naturally they were alarmed when the Nazis introduced laws that restricted the rights of all German-Jewish citizens. This was a foreshadowing of the terrible things yet to come. As the Nazis rose to power, many German Jews emigrated to other European countries and the Americas. Among them was Albert Einstein.

The German army crumbled, and the war in Europe was essentially over on May 8, 1945. The Allied soldiers were unprepared for what they found in the concentration camps at

At the time of the Olympic Games of 1936, Adolf Hitler was promulgating his theory of the master race. Jesse Owens (left) won three gold medals and obviously disproved Hitler's racial theory. The opening ceremony of the games (below) prominently featured the Nazi swastika.

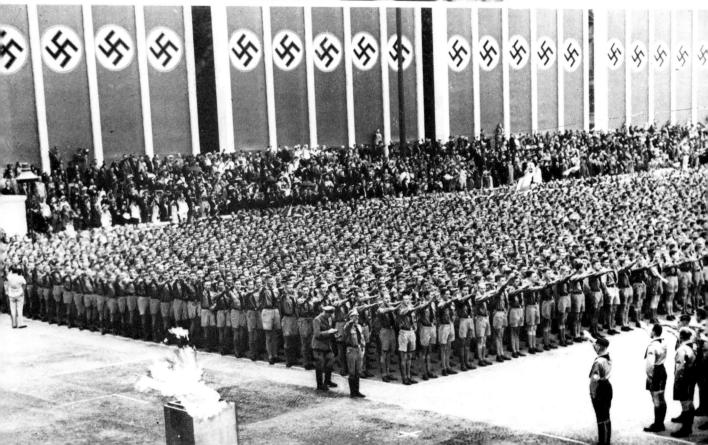

A rabbi who survived imprisonment in many detention camps arrives in America to start a new life with his family.

Auschwitz, Belsen, Buchenwald, and elsewhere. Six million Jews were murdered for no reason other than that they were Jews.

People have wondered how such atrocities could have been committed. The answers are myriad. But most people agree that the Holocaust really began when Jews were first denied their basic civil rights as German citizens. Without legal protection from law-enforcement agencies, Jews became victims of terrible crimes. The Nazis felt free to institute a program of genocide.

Many Holocaust survivors came to the United States, where they became outspoken civil rights advocates.

EXECUTIVE ORDER NO. 8802

At the same time that Jews were losing their rights in Europe, black Americans were struggling for their rights in America.

By 1938 Europe was at war, and it was just a matter of time before the United States also would be. The United States was in the process of a gigantic arms buildup. Yet employment opportunities for blacks remained limited. In January 1941 black leaders met with Roosevelt and presented their list of grievances.

Black machine gunners of the Fifth Army prepare for battle against the German forces in Italy near the end of World War II.

The spokesman for the group was A. Philip Randolph, president of the Brotherhood of Sleeping Car Porters. If their demands were not met, Randolph said that he was prepared to bring together "ten-twenty-fifty thousand Negroes on the White House lawn." Randolph was supported by other civil rights leaders.

Neither President Roosevelt nor his aides were able to change the black leaders' minds. After carefully considering the demands, the president issued Executive Order No. 8802 on June 25, 1941, calling for fair employment practices. "There shall be no discrimination in the employment of workers in defense industries and in Government, because of race, creed, color, or national origin."

Over the next three years, the order was followed up with the Committee on Fair Employment Practices. Training programs were set up to prepare black workers to qualify for employment.

The armed forces remained segregated throughout World War II. The highest ranking black officer was Brigadier General Benjamin O. Davis, Sr. His son, Benjamin O. Davis, Jr., who had graduated from West Point Military Academy, was serving in the United States Air Force.

THE JAPANESE INTERNMENT

On December 7, 1941, Japanese aircraft attacked the American fleet at Pearl Harbor in Hawaii. The United States was in a state of war.

On the West Coast, angry mobs attacked Japanese-American homes and businesses and looted, destroyed, and burned property. Often the attackers did not care whether or not the person was of Japanese descent. Anybody who "looked Oriental" was subjected to beatings and harassment.

Japanese-Americans who had lived in the United States for two or three generations were fired from jobs, dismissed from schools, and denied entry into American businesses.

The Federal Bureau of Investigation (FBI) rounded up about fifteen hundred Japanese-Americans who were considered a threat to American security. But someone decided that *all* people of Japanese descent were a threat. During the winter of 1942, the president signed an executive order that gave the army authority to evacuate " 'any and all persons' from 'military areas' as designated by the army and to provide 'accommodations' for them elsewhere."

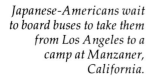

Japanese-Americans wait to board buses to take them from Los Angeles to a camp at Manzaner, California.

The first warning card posted in Los Angeles notifying enemy aliens to evacuate the prohibited areas

Japanese-Americans were not specified, but they were the only ones rounded up en masse—one hundred thousand men, women, and children—and taken to internment camps in isolated, barren regions in the interior of the United States.

General J. L. DeWitt, who was placed in charge of the internment, stated, "A Jap's a Jap, and it makes no difference whether he is a citizen or not." This is a clear indication of the mentality that governed the day. DeWitt's actions, sanctioned by the government, were motivated more by racism than by the interests of national security. The executive order was declared illegal by the Civil Liberties Union but was upheld by the Supreme Court. Yet not one Japanese-American was ever convicted of a single act of sabotage during the war years.

Life in the camps was depressing, nearly unbearable. While the Japanese-Americans were interned, their homes were sold, their property seized, and their businesses liquidated. Losses have been estimated at over $400 million. These were American citizens, not Japanese people who only happened to be living in the United States. If they were a threat, the question has been asked, why were Americans of German and Italian descent not rounded up en masse as well?

The 442nd Regiment of Japanese-Americans who fought in Europe during World War II

In January 1943 some Japanese-American men were allowed to join the military. The response was overwhelming because it gave them the opportunity to prove their loyalty to the country. More than three hundred thousand Japanese-Americans served in the war in segregated units. The 442d Regiment served in Europe and emerged as the most decorated combat unit in World War II. They suffered thousands of casualties in action against Nazi troops and earned fifty-two Distinguished Service Crosses and a Congressional Medal of Honor. In the Pacific several thousand Japanese-Americans served as interpreters and helped to break enemy codes.

THE TRUMAN YEARS (1945-1952)

Franklin Roosevelt was reelected for a fourth term in 1944. But he died on April 12, 1945, of a cerebral hemorrhage. Roosevelt was loved by some and hated by others. But all Americans paused to give respect to their deceased president. It was a sad and fearful time for a nation that was still at war.

Poor people—blacks and whites—mourned Roosevelt's death. For black Americans it was a personal loss. It was comforting to know that the numerous social programs he had started were still being funded. No other president had done so much for the needy. For this they were grateful. Poor people, blacks, and women remained loyal to the Democratic party for years after Roosevelt's death.

Just as the former slaves had worried after Lincoln's death, blacks worried again. What was Harry S. Truman from Independence, Missouri, going to do? He had served in the Senate, but he had only been vice-president for less than three months. Who was he? People were apprehensive at first. Although ill-prepared, Truman proved to be a capable and responsible president. And in 1945 he had some tough decisions to make.

President Truman had the atomic bomb. The question was, Should he use it? After carefully considering the pros and the cons, the president gave the order.

On August 6, 1945, a U.S. B-29 bomber dropped the first atomic bomb on Hiroshima, Japan. Three days later another was dropped on Nagasaki, Japan. On August 14, 1945, World War II was over. The question since then has been: should an atomic bomb ever be dropped again?

The Military Is Integrated

After World War II, it was "two steps backward" again. Racial discrimination increased; blacks were still the last to be hired and the first to be fired. Public accommodations, schools, parks, and

transportation were segregated, and in the South there were still lynchings. It was particularly difficult for the black soldier to receive this kind of reception.

James Baldwin wrote about the feelings of a black soldier who returned "home" after the war:

You must put yourself in the skin of a man who is wearing the uniform of his country, is a candidate for death in its defense, and who is called a "nigger" by his comrades-in-arms and his officers . . . and who watches German prisoners of war being treated by Americans with more human dignity than he has ever received at their hands. And who, at the same time, as a human being, is far freer in a strange land than he has ever been at home. HOME! The very word begins to have a despairing and diabolical ring. You must consider what happens to this citizen, after all he has endured, when he returns—home; search, in his shoes, for a job, for a place to live; ride, in his skin, on segregated buses; see, with his eyes, the signs saying "White" and "Colored," and especially the signs that say "White Ladies" and "Colored Women"; . . . imagine yourself being told to "Wait."

Black people were running out of patience. They were tired of waiting.

A. Philip Randolph and other black leaders planned a massive protest against the draft unless the military was integrated. President Truman met with the group and accepted their demands. The president agreed that what they were asking was reasonable and right. So he integrated the U.S. military against the advice of General Dwight D. Eisenhower.

North Korean communist troops invaded South Korea in June 1950. Under the command of General Douglas MacArthur, U.S. forces joined soldiers from other countries to form the United Nations Force.

During the Korean War, the U.S. military was integrated for the first time in history, and black officers were placed in command of integrated combat units.

The Civil Rights Commission

During Truman's administration, literacy tests for voting were declared unconstitutional, and border states began token desegration of graduate schools and universities. Segregated parties on the state level (called "white primaries") were outlawed, and the armed forces were integrated. Those were important advances.

But it was the appointment of the Civil Rights Commission that gave black people a feeling that something substantial was about to be done. One year after the commission had been appointed, they presented a document to the president. It outlined how the government had failed to protect the civil rights of all citizens in the United States. The following is a summary of what the report recommended.

President Truman receiving a report from the special Committee on Civil Rights. Left to right are: Reverend Francis J. Haas; Rabbi Roland G. Gittelsohn; Mrs. M.E. Tilly; Channing H. Tobias (partially hidden); Charles E. Wilson, chairman, making the presentation; Boris Shiskin; Charles Luckman, and Francis P. Matthews.

To Secure These Rights

1. The reorganization of the Civil Rights Section of the Department of Justice to provide for:

    The establishment of regional offices;

    A substantial increase in its appropriation and staff to enable it to engage in more extensive research and to act more effectively to prevent civil rights violations;

    An increase in investigative action in the absence of complaints;

    The greater use of civil sanctions;

    Its elevation to the status of a full division in the Department of Justice.

2. The establishment within the FBI of a special unit of investigators trained in civil rights work.

Senator Joseph McCarthy discusses the Communist party in America. Seated is Joseph N. Welch, an army counsel, who had just denounced McCarthy as a "cruelly reckless character assassin."

3. The establishment by the state governments of law enforcement agencies comparable to the federal Civil Rights Section.

4. The establishment of a permanent Commission on Civil Rights in the Executive Office of the President, preferably by Act of Congress;
And the simultaneous creation of a Joint Standing Committee on Civil Rights in Congress.

5. The establishment by the states of permanent commissions on civil rights to parallel the work of the federal Commission at the state level.

6. The increased professionalization of state and local police forces.

Half of the proposals were not put into effect but much of the civil rights legislation that was passed between 1957 and 1975 used this report as a model.

McCARTHYISM

Joseph McCarthy, a senator from Wisconsin, made the statement that the army and "State Department was thoroughly infested with Communists." That started a witch-hunt, beginning in 1950, that violated the rights of countless American people.

The frenzied period known as the McCarthy Era began with investigations conducted within the government. The search for Communist infiltrators spread into the community at large. People lost their heads and began accusing people of being Communists without proof that they were. On the hearsay evidence of one or two individuals, people lost their jobs, their homes, and their families. Writers, ministers, actors, businessmen, teachers, and students were branded Communists, driven out of communities, and forced to live as outcasts.

In the spring of 1949, W.E.B. DuBois and Paul Robeson, a controversial black musician, predicted the spread of socialism in

Paul Robeson singing at a rally in Philadelphia

Third World countries and among oppressed people because of the dehumanizing oppression of colonial and capitalistic societies.

The anticommunism tide that was rising in America was not tolerant of these ideas, especially those spoken by black men. DuBois was suddenly a man without a past or a future. All the work he had done in the past was canceled. Atlanta University and the NAACP disassociated themselves from him. By then, DuBois was old, frustrated, and very tired. He offered no defense. When black people shunned him, he gave up the struggle completely. His passport was revoked, and for a long while he was denied international travel. Later he was permitted to leave. Leaving America a bitter but proud man, he lived the rest of his life in France and Africa, where he lectured and wrote.

Finally, Joseph McCarthy was censured by his colleagues in the Senate by a vote of 76 to 22, condemning him for his arrogance and intolerance. He died in Bethesda, Maryland, in 1957. But how many innocent people had suffered because of his excessive misuse of power?

BROWN V. TOPEKA: A GIANT LEAP FOR CIVIL RIGHTS

General Dwight D. Eisenhower, commander of the Allied forces in Europe during World War II, was elected president in 1952. President Eisenhower was not known for being a supporter of civil rights. Yet one of the strongest advances in civil rights history was made in the second year of the Eisenhower administration.

The *Plessy v. Ferguson* doctrine of "separate but equal," which had supported segregation in the United States since 1896, was shattered in the *Brown v. Topeka* case. Jim Crow was on the run.

Cameos

CARRIE CHAPMAN CATT

Carrie Chapman Catt was born in 1859. In 1900 she became the president of the National American Woman Suffrage Association and fought for woman suffrage until the Nineteenth Amendment was ratified in 1920.

Carrie Catt also helped start the Daughters of the American Revolution (DAR). Members were required to present proof that one of their ancestors was a Revolutionary War patriot. Yet a direct descendant of Crispus Attucks, a black hero in the Boston Massacre, was not allowed to belong to the DAR.

JAMES WELDON JOHNSON

James Weldon Johnson was a poet, novelist, scholar, diplomat, and civil rights leader in the first two decades of the twentieth century.

Johnson was the first black to pass the bar examination in the state of Florida. He distinguished himself as a writer before taking up other pursuits.

During the Wilson administration, Johnson served as consul to Nicaragua and Venezuela. In 1916 Johnson became the executive secretary of the NAACP, a post he held for many years. Working with DuBois, he helped get the Dyer Anti-Lynching Bill passed in 1921.

But James Weldon Johnson is best remembered for his famous poem "Lift Every Voice and Sing." It was set to music, and it became the "black anthem."

HIDEYO NOGUCHI (1876-1928)

Hideyo Noguchi was Japanese. He developed a method to detect congenital syphilis, a venereal disease. His research was used to treat Rocky Mountain spotted fever, yellow fever, and snakebite.

America cannot claim this outstanding scientist. Because of his race, Noguchi was not permitted to become an American citizen, although he lived in the United States all his life.

BLACK RENAISSANCE POETS AND THEIR WORK

The work created by black poets in the 1920s was full of humor, sadness, hope, and anger. These two examples reflect the wide range of styles and emotions present in the Renaissance writing of blacks.

CLAUDE McKAY

McKay was a Jamaican who attended Tuskegee Institute in 1912. He began his writing career during the Red Summer of 1919.

If We Must Die

If we must die—let it not be like hogs
Hunted and penned in an inglorious spot,
While round us bark the mad and hungry dogs,
Making their mock at our accursed lot.
If we must die—oh, let us nobly die,
So that our precious blood may not be shed
In vain; then even the monsters we defy
Shall be constrained to honor us though dead!
Oh, Kinsmen! We must meet the common foe;
Though far outnumbered, let us show us brave,
And for their thousand blows deal one deathblow!
What though before us lies the open grave?
Like men we'll face the murderous, cowardly pack,
Pressed to the wall, dying, but fight back!

COUNTEE CULLEN

Cullen was born in New York, the son of a Methodist minister. He is best remembered for his sharp images and cutting wit.

For A Lady I Know

She even thinks that up in heaven
    Her class lies late and snores,
While poor black cherubs rise at seven
    To do celestial chores.

WILLIAM MONROE TROTTER

William Monroe Trotter was a handsome, young Harvard honor graduate from a well-to-do Boston family. His positions often placed him in conflict with Booker T. Washington and W.E.B. DuBois. Trotter resented Washington's "let it alone" philosophy regarding civil rights and refused to work with interracial groups because he felt that they were too moderate.

Trotter was the owner of the newspaper *The Guardian* and helped to set its editorial policy, which, in the early 1900s, was considered militant. He died in 1934 under "mysterious circumstances" at the age of sixty-two.

THE REAL McCOY (1843-1929)

Elijah McCoy, a black man, invented automatic lubrication devices that eliminated the need to shut down large machinery to lubricate it. At this time children had to oil equipment in factories, and that is how so many were hurt. McCoy's invention probably saved the lives and limbs of many children.

When people wanted one of his machines, they wanted to know if it was a "real McCoy." That's how the phrase entered our language.

A. PHILIP RANDOLPH

A. Philip Randolph was a spokesman for black labor. Black men worked for the railroad companies, but they had few rights as employees. In 1925 Randolph founded the all-black Brotherhood of Sleeping Car Porters. He was attacked by railroad management but held on until the union was formed.

Randolph remained in the forefront of the struggle for civil rights through the 1960s. In the end Randolph earned the respect of management and labor because he never yielded or compromised for personal gain.

CHARLES RICHARD DREW

Charles Drew saved thousands of lives with his research in preserving whole-blood plasma. He was the first director of the American Red Cross Blood Bank during World War II.

Ironically, he died at the age of forty-five because after an auto accident he was refused help at a "white" hospital in North Carolina. A blood transfusion might have saved his life.

THE CODE TALKERS

During World War II, Navaho Indian marines used their language to send coded messages for the military. The American forces had the only code in the history of warfare that could not be decoded. The Navaho language baffled the enemy.

MARIAN ANDERSON

Marian Anderson is one of America's leading contraltos. She was the first black woman to sing at the Metropolitan Opera.

During the Roosevelt administration, the DAR denied Anderson the right to sing at Constitution Hall. Eleanor Roosevelt, the first lady, resigned from the organization and made arrangements for Marian Anderson to sing at the Lincoln Memorial. Seventy-five thousand people came to hear her sing there in 1939.

ELEANOR ROOSEVELT

Mrs. Roosevelt was a champion of the poor and oppressed people everywhere in the world. She was active in the NAACP and other organizations that advanced the cause of freedom and justice. She integrated White House gatherings and included people from all ethnic groups in state functions. For this she was highly criticized.

After President Roosevelt's death, the first lady continued her work and served as the first U.S. ambassador to the United Nations.

PAUL ROBESON

Although he is known best as a musician and political activist, Paul Robeson was a star athlete at Rutgers University. He also was an honor student, graduating at the top of his class at Columbia University Law School.

His wife encouraged him to audition for a role in a musical. He did, and that launched his career as one of the world's greatest baritones.

Paul Robeson was outspoken against racism in America and often made pro-Communist statements that made him a target of the House Un-American Activities Committee. From 1950 to 1958 his passport was revoked, and he was prevented from giving concerts. That still did not silence his voice against lynchings, segregation, job discrimination, and other injustices.

JIM THORPE

Jim Thorpe was a Sac and Fox American Indian who was born in 1888. He has been called one of the greatest all-around athletes in the world. There is an interesting story behind this famous athlete.

In the 1912 Olympics, Thorpe won gold medals in the decathlon and the pentathlon. That means that he competed in fifteen different events and outscored all his challengers.

Thorpe had received room and board while playing baseball the summer before the Olympics. He did not report it because he did not take any actual money. The Olympic Committee was informed, and he was disqualified on the basis that he was a professional. Both his medals were revoked, and his name was stricken from the record books.

In his lifetime Thorpe played professional baseball for the New York Giants as well as professional football.

In 1920 he was the first president of the American Football Association, which later became the National Football League.

Thorpe fought the Olympic decision throughout his lifetime. Even after his death in 1953, his children and grandchildren continued to petition the Olympic Committee; finally, the decision was reversed. Today Jim Thorpe is back in the record books, where he belongs.

MARY McLEOD BETHUNE

Mary McLeod Bethune was born in 1875. Her parents were South Carolina sharecroppers, but they wanted their first child born in freedom to get an education. They did not know at the time that Mary Bethune would become a college president and adviser to the president of the United States.

Mary Bethune got off a train in Daytona Beach, Florida, in 1902. All she had was $1.50, her son, and the desire to open a school for black children—and she did it. By 1923 the small school that she had built on land that had been the city dump was Bethune College. Bethune College merged with Cookman College to become Bethune-Cookman College, which is still in existence today.

During his first term as president, Franklin D. Roosevelt appointed Mrs. Bethune the director of the Negro Affairs Division of the National Youth Administration. She was always a welcomed visitor at the White House and served in the Roosevelt administration in several key positions. Mrs. Bethune was also an American delegate to the first United Nations conference.

THE JOURNAL

OF

NEGRO HISTORY

CARTER G. WOODSON

EDITOR

VOLUME I

1916

THE ASSOCIATION FOR THE STUDY OF NEGRO LIFE
AND HISTORY, Inc.
LANCASTER, PA., AND WASHINGTON, D. C.
1916

CARTER WOODSON

Carter Woodson was born in 1875 in Canton, Virginia. His family could not afford schooling, so he worked as a coal miner to earn the money for his education. Woodson was graduated from high school at the age of twenty-two and went to colleges in Kentucky and Illinois. He received his Ph.D. in philosophy from Harvard University in 1912 at the age of thirty-eight.

Woodson was concerned that books written about blacks were inaccurate and racially biased. Many of the history books that were written at that time eliminated black Americans' contributions. So in 1915 Woodson organized the Association for the Study of Negro Life and History. A few of his many books include *The Education of the Negro Prior to 1861, A Century of Negro Migration, The Negro in Our History, Negro Makes History*, and *The History of the Negro Church*.

Carter Woodson began the observances of Negro History Week in 1927 to help make information available to the public about black American history. Woodson was a cofounder of the *Negro History Bulletin*, a journal that published black scholarly research about black Americans.

BENJAMIN O. DAVIS, SR. AND BENJAMIN O. DAVIS, JR.

In 1940 President Franklin Roosevelt promoted Benjamin O. Davis, Sr., to the rank of brigadier (one-star) general. General Davis was near retirement age when he became the first black general in the history of the U.S. military.

Twenty-five years later, Benjamin O. Davis, Jr., following his father's footsteps, was promoted to lieutenant general, making him the first officer to reach that rank in the U.S. Air Force.

General Davis, Jr., had an unusual military record, which began at West Point Military Academy in 1932. Because he was black, Davis was given the silent treatment—none of his classmates spoke to him socially. He was completely alone and without friends for four years. Most cadets could not endure being isolated and alone, but Davis endured the ordeal and earned the respect of all those who had tried to break him.

After graduation from West Point in 1936, Davis wanted to join the U.S. Air Force, but his request was denied because he was black. When the all-black Ninety-ninth Pursuit Squadron was formed, Davis was allowed to become a pilot. During World War II, Colonel Davis was an outstanding commander and won numerous awards, among them the Silver Star. President Lyndon Johnson promoted Davis to lieutenant general in 1964.

LANGSTON HUGHES

Langston Hughes ranks among America's greatest writers. He emerged as one of the most prolific and well-known of the Harlem Renaissance writers. Hughes wrote about ordinary people that he met while busing tables to earn a living and about those he met during his travels many years later. "Simple" was one of Hughes's most engaging characters, whose ordinary ideas gave the reader something to think about once they stopped laughing.

Hughes was born in Joplin, Missouri, in 1902 and died at the age of sixty-five, leaving the world a treasury of poems, biographies, plays, novels, and songs.

JAPANESE-AMERICAN PATRIOTISM

In The Glory and the Dream, the author William Manchester describes the Japanese internment:

Surrounded by barbed wire, with powerful searchlights in watchtowers sweeping their windows each night, they struggled to recapture something of the life they had known before Pearl Harbor, teaching the children, holding church services, and attending what eventually turned out to be 2,120 marriages, 5,981 christenings, and 1,862 funerals.

In the midst of this, the Japanese-Americans were described as being patriotic. Manchester said,

To the confusion of their guards, they assembled each morning to raise the Stars and Stripes and salute it while their Boy Scout drum and bugle corps (every camp had one) played the national anthem. At Camp Topaz 3,250 adults were enrolled in camp courses; the two most popular were the English language and American history. Saturday evenings they sang "America the Beautiful. . ."

A Japanese family eating dinner in a large mess hall at a detention center during World War II.

HUDDLED MASSES . . .

The term "huddled masses" comes from the inscription on the base of the Statue of Liberty. These five lines are an excerpt from a longer poem that was written by Emma Lazarus:

Give me your tired, your poor,
Your huddled masses yearning to breathe free,
The wretched refuse of your teeming shore.
Send these, the homeless, tempest-tost to me.
I lift my lamp beside the golden door!

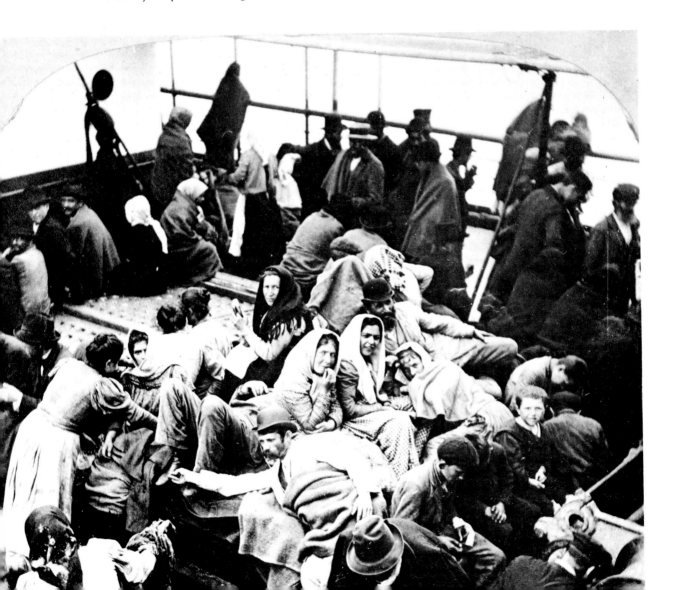

Eight of the nine accused in the Scottsboro *case*

THE *SCOTTSBORO* CASE

Two white girls, hoboing their way through the South in 1931, accused nine blacks from Scottsboro, Alabama, aged twelve to nineteen, of rape. The black youths were tried and convicted by an all-white jury.

William Pikens, field secretary of the NAACP, wrote about the case in 1933:

For generations in this country when a Negro came into court facing a white opponent, he had to settle not only the question involved in the charge against him as an individual, but also all the traditional charges against his race — in fact the whole "race question." Like Socrates before his accusers, he had to face a jury which was influenced not only by the evidence just presented, but also by the "evidence" that had been taught to them in their infancy, in their growing up, in literature, taverns, shops, and from a million other sources.

Two members of the Ninety-ninth Pursuit Squadron, Lemuel R. Custis and Charles B. Hall

BLACK WINGS OVER AMERICA

The Ninety-ninth Pursuit Squadron, also known as the Tuskegee Airmen, were an all-black flying unit during World War II. They were trained at an air base built in Tuskegee, Alabama, specifically to train black pilots.

The Ninety-ninth flew 3,277 combat missions in Europe, and eighty members of the unit won the Distinguished Flying Cross. The 332nd Fighter Group was combined with the Ninety-ninth Pursuit Squadron under the command of Colonel Benjamin O. Davis, Jr. The 332nd was awarded the Distinguished Unit Citation for its sixteen-hundred-mile round-trip air attack on Berlin on March 24, 1945.

Roger Baldwin, founder of the American Civil Liberties Union

AMERICAN CIVIL LIBERTIES UNION

The American Civil Liberties Union (ACLU) was founded in 1920 to defend "the rights of man set forth in the Declaration of Independence." The ACLU legally defends any person whose rights, guaranteed by the Constitution, have been denied. It does not matter how unpopular the person or his or her position may be. For example, the ACLU has defended both civil rights workers and Ku Klux Klan members.

The ACLU was very vocal against the internment of Japanese Americans during World War II, calling it "the worst single wholesale violation of civil rights of American citizens in our history." That was a very unpopular opinion at the time. The organization's most unpopular case in recent years was the defense of a neo-Nazi group that had been denied a march permit in the town of Skokie, Illinois, a mainly Jewish community. The ACLU argued and won the case. The court ruled that, according to the Constitution, the neo-Nazis had a legal right to conduct a public march.

The ACLU is supported by two hundred thousand members who help sponsor hundreds of cases each year.

THE AFL-CIO

The American Federation of Labor (AFL) was organized in 1886 at a trade union convention in Columbus, Ohio. Samuel Gompers served as the organization's president until his death in 1924. The AFL represented skilled workers such as carpenters, bricklayers, stonecutters, and other craftsmen. The AFL fought for the rights of workers—safer working conditions, reasonable hours, and better wages. Black craftsmen belonged to segregated locals of separate unions. Women were not included.

The Congress of Industrial Organization (CIO) was formed in 1935 as a committee within the AFL. The purpose of the CIO committee was to unionize factory workers and to improve working conditions. In 1936 there was a dispute over authority, and the CIO broke from the AFL and became a separate union that represented automobile, textile, rubber, electric, and mine workers. John L. Lewis was the CIO's first president, and he welcomed blacks, other minorities, and women, but they were members of segregated locals.

At the time, the CIO was considered a militant group because its leaders readily used strikes instead of long and often unproductive negotiations. They also fought to pass child-labor laws, minimum wages, and the restriction of the employment of youths in factories.

In 1955 the AFL and the CIO united. George Meany was the first president of the consolidated union. Many of the AFL-CIO locals remained segregated, but the national organization elected minorities and women to management positions.

BROWN V. TOPEKA (KANSAS)

The NAACP had been testing the legality of the 1896 *Plessy v. Ferguson* Supreme Court decision since the organization began. In 1954 the NAACP sponsored taking the *Brown v. Topeka* case to the Supreme Court. Thurgood Marshall, lawyer for the NAACP, presented the arguments for Brown.

On May 17, 1954, Justice Earl Warren presented the decision of the Court:

Segregation of white and colored children in public schools has a detrimental effect upon the colored children. The impact is greater when it has the sanction of the law; for the policy of separating the races is usually interpreted as denoting the inferiority of the negro group. A sense of inferiority affects the motivation of a child to learn. Segregation with the sanction of law, therefore, has a tendency to [retard] the educational and mental development of negro children and to deprive them of some of the benefits they would receive in a racial[ly] integrated school system.

The justices concluded that "in the field of public education the doctrine of 'separate but equal' has no place."

The victorious lawyers in the Brown v. Topeka *case are, left to right; George E.C. Hayes, Thurgood Marshall, and James M. Nabrit.*

The first meeting of the United Nations in San Francisco

THE UNITED NATIONS DECLARATION OF HUMAN RIGHTS

The Holocaust and the atomic and hydrogen bombs made the world recognize the importance of human rights. When the nations of the world met in San Francisco to form the United Nations, three black Americans were included in the U.S. delegation: Walter White, executive secretary of the NAACP; W.E.B. DuBois; and Mary McLeod Bethune, former presidential adviser. Eleanor Roosevelt, the widow of the former president, was also an American delegate. She was elected to chair the commission that was responsible for drafting the international bill of rights.

This, then, is a portion of the Charter of the United Nations:

We the Peoples of the United Nations . . . reaffirm faith in fundamental human rights, in the dignity and worth of the human person, in the equal rights of men and women and of nations large and small . . . and respect for human rights and for fundamental freedoms for all without distinction as to race, sex, language, or religion.

It was adopted on December 10, 1948. At the time that the document was being accepted, black Americans, Hispanics, Asians, and Jews were being discriminated against in the United States.

PRESIDENTS FROM 1901 TO 1954

Theodore Roosevelt	1901-09
William H. Taft	1909-13
Woodrow Wilson	1913-21
Warren G. Harding	1921-23
Calvin Coolidge	1923-29
Herbert Hoover	1929-33
Franklin D. Roosevelt	1933-45
Harry S. Truman	1945-53
Dwight D. Eisenhower	1953-61

THEODORE ROOSEVELT

WILLIAM H. TAFT

WOODROW WILSON

WARREN G. HARDING

CALVIN COOLIDGE

HERBERT HOOVER

FRANKLIN D. ROOSEVELT

HARRY S. TRUMAN

DWIGHT D. EISENHOWER

Part III

Climbing to the Mountaintop

TIME LINE 1955-1964

1955   Rosa Parks defies a Jim Crow law, followed by Montgomery bus boycott led by Martin Luther King, Jr., and local NAACP leaders

1957   The Civil Rights Act of 1957; Little Rock school crisis; Martin Luther King, Jr., and Ralph Abernathy help form Southern Christian Leadership Conference (SCLC); first march on Washington

1958   King writes book *Stride Toward Freedom;* assassination attempt made on King's life

1960   John F. Kennedy wins presidential election; Robert Kennedy appointed attorney general; first sit-ins held in Greensboro, North Carolina

1961   Freedom rides; Voter registration drives; Students for Nonviolent Coordinating Committee formed (SNCC); Nonviolent peaceful protests throughout southern region

1963   Birmingham confrontation with Bull Connor; march on Washington; Birmingham church bombing; President John F. Kennedy assassinated; Lyndon B. Johnson becomes president

1964   President Johnson pushes for passage of the Civil Rights Bill; Martin Luther King, Jr., wins Nobel Peace Prize; Malcolm X breaks from Elijah Muhammad's Muslim sect; Lyndon Johnson is elected president

Oh beautiful, for spacious skies | For amber waves of grain | For purple mountains majesty | Above the fruited plain | America, America | God shed Thy grace on th...

One of the major domestic political issues between 1955 and 1960 was school desegregation.

1955-1964

SCHOOL DESEGREGATION

School desegregation was the major domestic political issue between 1955 and 1960. Oliver Brown's eight-year-old daughter traveled twenty-one blocks to school, even though there was a school less than two blocks away. The school around the corner was an all-white school—no black children were allowed. The whole concept was ludicrous. With the help of the NAACP, Brown sued the Topeka, Kansas, school board, which led to the *Brown v. Topeka* Supreme Court decision of 1954.

Yet in the fall of 1955, southern schools were still functioning under the "separate but unequal" system. Black children traveled miles to poorly equipped, understaffed, and overcrowded facilities. They very often had to share books because there were not enough for every student. But down the street, white students had every convenience. Since the school boards and school administrations remained all white, the system could not be changed from within.

The year after the *Brown* decision, the Supreme Court ruled that schools should be integrated "with all deliberate speed." What did that mean? Unfortunately, segregationists interpreted it to mean "take all the time you need." Since no date was given, states could set their own deadlines for integration. "Oh, we'll get around to it in the year 2000," southern politicians said smugly. Desegregation of schools was delayed indefinitely by many districts.

Earl Warren (left) was Chief Justice of the Supreme Court from 1953 to 1969. Hubert H. Humphrey (right) was a senator from Minnesota and vice president of the United States from 1965 to 1969.

Some commentators believe that the delay was caused because President Eisenhower did not send a clear message to the South that he supported the Supreme Court's decision. In fact, the president declined to endorse the *Brown* decision, saying that he would neither approve nor disapprove it. "Feelings are deep on this," said the president. "And the fellow who tries to tell me that you can do these things by force is just plain nuts." Then he publicly denounced his appointment of Justice Earl Warren, saying that it was "the biggest . . . fool mistake I ever made."

Hubert Humphrey, who was a senator from Minnesota at the

time, was critical of Eisenhower's actions regarding the *Brown* decision. He later wrote,

> The first reaction to the decision among segregationists had been rather mild and resigned: they would, after all, have to obey the law. In border states and the District of Columbia many school districts were soon integrated. But gradually opposition mounted and hardened. . . . The period between the Supreme Court's decision of May, 1954, and the Little Rock crisis of September, 1957, should have been a time for strong initiative by the federal government to underline the necessity for obedience to law and the firm commitment by the executive to enforce it. But it was not.

The leading Democrat and presidential candidate, Adlai Stevenson, did not differ too much from President Eisenhower on the issue. Stevenson also advocated gradualism and the "take it slow" approach to desegregation.

Some school districts in Missouri, Kansas, Indiana, and parts of West Virginia and Maryland quietly integrated. Although a few superintendents, principals, and teachers resigned rather than work in integrated school systems, other willing educators took their places, and the gap closed quickly. The transitions were made without major incidents. In the Deep South it was another story. White leadership encouraged their people to resist segregation. First, there were the endless rounds of debates and arguments. When that failed, they used force and violence to obstruct justice.

White citizens' councils were formed overnight. Unscientific reports were issued that concluded that black children were inferior to white children. The governor of Alabama defied a court order by denying Miss Autherine Lucy and other black students admission to the state university at Tuscaloosa. A local judge stated, "Autherine is just one unfortunate girl who doesn't know

Autherine Lucy is in the center (without a hat).

what she is doing, but in Montgomery it looks like all the niggers have gone crazy."

On March 12, 1956, 101 southern members of Congress signed a "declaration of Constitution principles," asking states to disobey the desegregation order. Southerners believed that only states had the power to decide whether a school should be segregated. The manifesto was signed by all but three southern senators: Lyndon B. Johnson from Texas and Estes Kefauver and Albert Gore from Tennessee.

Other techniques were used to stall school desegregation. With the philosophy of "as long as we can legislate, we can segregate," state legislatures passed 450 laws to keep public schools from becoming integrated. Some of those states' laws forced the disclosure of NAACP membership. Members were fired from jobs and harassed. All this lawless behavior went unchecked for over three years, but it helped to galvanize public sentiment against segregation, especially among young people.

Martin Luther King, Jr. calls on the government to put more guts into the Supreme Court's desegregation decisions.

THE CIVIL RIGHTS ACT OF 1957

Eisenhower was reelected for a second term in November 1956 with the support of the black population. The president continued to call for moderation on both sides of the civil rights issues. He asked blacks to "go slow." He advised southerners to be more flexible. But segregationists had shown that they were not going to give an inch without force regarding desegregation. And black people were no longer willing to wait for rights that were already theirs by law.

The momentum seemed to be moving in favor of blacks. Public opinion was shifting toward more liberal civil rights legislation. A civil rights act was passed and signed in 1957. The bill called for: the establishment of a special Civil Rights Division within the Department of Justice; the creation of a Federal Civil Rights Commission to study the status of civil rights in the nation and make recommendations for legislation; authority for the Department of Justice to intervene, in the name of the United States, in behalf of individuals in instances of actual or threatened violations of general civil rights, such as the right to attend an integrated school; and similar authorization for federal intervention against violations of the right to vote.

A few black leaders criticized the Civil Rights Act of 1957 for being too mild. Roy Wilkins, the director of the NAACP, summed up the attitude of black leadership at the time: "If you are digging a ditch with a teaspoon, and a man comes along and offers you a spade, there is something wrong with your head if you don't take it because he didn't offer you a bulldozer."

Two years later, the Civil Rights Commission's report was submitted. Another report was submitted in 1961. The 1959 commission recommended that Congress "abolish literacy tests in all elections; that legislation be adopted requiring every local school board that still maintained segregated schools to file a desegregation plan within six months; that federal laws be enacted providing strengthened criminal sanctions against lawful official violence and subjecting local governments to liability for unlawful acts of its officers."

Black people were amazed that it took two years to come up with such obvious recommendations. Still, black and white leaders counseled patience.

THE LITTLE ROCK CRISIS

Arkansas was not considered a state of the Deep South. There had even been some steps made to desegregate schools there in 1956. However, that year Governor Orval Faubus was nominated for a third term. He knew it was going to be a hard-fought battle to win, so he used the southern political strategy known as "out-niggering." (This term seems to have been coined when George Wallace ran for office as a "moderate." After losing the election, he was quoted as saying, "They outniggered me this time, but they'll never do it again.") In the South it was generally a rule that the candidate who capitalized on racism, fear, and ignorance

Governor Orval Faubus (right) announced he would not be responsible for
any violence that might occur if black students entered Central High School
in Little Rock. Elizabeth Echford (left) calmly marches to the main entrance
of Central High School while white students shout at her.

usually won. Orval Faubus promised never to allow integration in
the state of Arkansas and won the election.

Nine black students were scheduled to enroll at all-white
Central High School in Little Rock in September 1957. According
to reports from the school board, the decision to integrate had not
met with much resistance.

On September 2, 1957, Faubus appeared on local television to
announce that he would not be responsible for the violence that
would follow if the nine black students tried to enter Central
High. Actually, no violence had been expected. But the seed had
been planted. Faubus ordered the National Guard to the school.
His plan was effective. The nine black students stayed away.

The federal district court quickly issued a court order. The
governor was asked to stop interfering with the school board's
desegregation plan. The next day, an all-white crowd gathered
outside the school. Adults carried abusive signs and yelled
obscenities. One woman said that her daddy would turn over in
his grave if he knew niggers were going to school with his

grandson. She prayed it wouldn't happen. A Klan member melodramatically promised the sobbing woman that desegregation would happen only over his dead body.

As the world watched, the drama unfolded on nationwide television. The black students arrived at Central High. Under orders from the governor, the guardsmen blocked the students' entrance and did not permit them to enter. The crowd cheered its approval.

Governor Faubus, like the States' Righters in the past, had challenged the authority of the federal government. The world waited to see what the president would do. He chose to meet with Governor Faubus on September 14, 1957. Faubus interpreted the meeting as a sign of weakness and continued to disobey the court order, saying that he was defending the right of a state to handle matters regarding education.

On September 20 the federal district court repeated the order to stop interfering with school desegregation in Little Rock. Governor Faubus withdrew the National Guard from Central High and left the state.

When the nine black students arrived at Central High on the morning of September 23, 1957, over one thousand shrieking protesters surrounded the high school. White citizens' groups from across the South formed the mob; adults jeered, yelled, and screamed at the nine high school students. A cruel cheer was chanted: "Two, four, six, eight, we ain't gonna integrate."

Finally, the nine blacks were admitted inside the school from a side entrance; white students protested by leaving. They were welcomed by the cheering protesters. There was a bomb threat, so Little Rock's police commander had the black students withdrawn from the school.

That evening, President Eisenhower appeared on television and denounced the Little Rock incident. He ordered those who were interfering with school desegregation to "cease and desist."

The protesters responded by returning the next morning. It was a direct confrontation between state authority and the national government. Eisenhower was forced to act. Reluctantly, he used the power that had been given to President Andrew Jackson during the Nullification Crisis of 1832. Eisenhower federalized the National Guard and dispatched one thousand troops from the 101st Airborne Division. The next morning, paratroopers, some of whom were black, escorted the nine students into Central High School.

President Eisenhower explained his actions, saying that it was not for the sake of integration that the troops were sent in but rather to uphold national supremacy, defend presidential authority, and enforce the law of the land. But in so doing Eisenhower became the first president since Reconstruction to use armed troops to support the rights of black people. Still, rather than desegregate, some southern states closed their public schools. It would take countless court orders to open them again.

In the meantime, southern blacks were not going to wait for things to happen—they were taking action to secure their own rights. A movement was under way in Montgomery, Alabama, led by a young minister, the Reverend Dr. Martin Luther King, Jr.

ROSA PARKS

On December 1, 1955, Mrs. Rosa Parks boarded a bus. She had worked hard as a seamstress in a department store that day, so she was tired. She found a seat in the rear of the bus, where only blacks were expected to sit. Blacks were also expected to give their

Rosa Parks is fingerprinted in Montgomery.

seats to white passengers when seats up front were filled.

As the bus filled, a few white passengers were without seats, but Mrs. Parks remained seated. The bus driver stopped the bus. He ordered Mrs. Parks to give her seat to a white person who was standing nearby, but she refused, saying that she had paid to ride and had a *right* to be seated.

Mrs. Parks was a small, neatly dressed woman whose poise and quiet manner caught the bus driver off guard. She was not loud or boisterous, but she was firm. She was not going to give up her seat. The bus driver called the police, and Mrs. Parks was arrested and booked for violating a Montgomery, Alabama, city ordinance. She was released on bond.

When local leaders of the NAACP and other black organizations heard about Mrs. Parks' arrest, they rallied behind her. A one-day boycott was planned to protest the unfair city ordinance that made segregated buses legal. The NAACP felt that Mrs. Parks' case was one that they could take to the Supreme Court to test the legality of segregation laws on public facilities.

Black ministers were contacted all over Montgomery to help with the bus boycott. One minister who was called on for help was the young Dr. Martin Luther King, Jr., from Atlanta, Georgia.

Martin Luther King, Jr., had not been living in Montgomery long. He was the new minister at Dexter Avenue Baptist Church, as well as a new husband and father. Dr. King recalled a phrase from Henry David Thoreau's essay "Civil Disobedience," which reads "We can no longer lend our cooperation to an evil system." Dr. King believed that the boycott was morally right, and he felt obligated to be a part of it.

In 1955 forty-eight thousand blacks lived in Montgomery, and 75 percent used public transportation regularly. On the day of the boycott, December 5, 1955, only eight blacks were seen riding on a city bus. The organizers called it an overwhelming success.

Mrs. Parks appeared in court. She was fined fourteen dollars. Fred Gray, the NAACP lawyer who was representing Mrs. Parks, informed the judge that he would appeal the decision. That also was hailed a success.

THE MONTGOMERY BUS BOYCOTT

The successful one-day boycott had set an example. Spirits were running high. The Montgomery Improvement Association (MIA) was formed to be the permanent committee that would plan and carry out a longer bus boycott. Dr. Martin Luther King, Jr., was nominated and unanimously elected president of the MIA. As he graciously accepted the position, he told his supporters, "There will be no threats and intimidation. . . . Our actions must be guided by the deepest principles of our Christian faith. Love must be our regulating ideal.''

The MIA had three demands: (1) courteous treatment on buses; (2) seating on a first-come, first-served basis; and (3) black bus drivers on predominantly black routes. Montgomery blacks refused to ride public buses until their demands were met.

At first the boycott was ignored by city officials. But by the end of the first month, downtown businesses were beginning to feel their losses. The boycott was having a definite effect on downtown trade. White businessmen and local politicians tried threats, arrests, and outright violence. Still the boycott was not called off. Rather than ride the city buses, blacks formed car pools, walked, or stayed home.

Tempers flared, and people were angry. On January 30, 1956, Martin Luther King's house was bombed. His wife and daughter barely escaped. Many expected Dr. King to respond angrily.

Reverend Martin Luther King, Jr. and his wife, Coretta, stand among cheering supporters after Dr. King was convicted for taking part in the Montgomery bus boycott.

WHITE PASSENGERS
Please Fill Seats From Front of Car
COLORED PASSENGERS
From Rear

Signs used in buses in the South before segregation was outlawed

Instead, Dr. King said, "Remember, if I am stopped, this movement will not stop because God is with this movement." Those who heard him were amazed that he could speak with compassion at such a time. Those who saw him calm the angry crowd outside his home knew that he was no ordinary leader.

The Montgomery bus boycott was long and bitter. In the eleventh month of the protest, boycotters were tired of being harassed, fined, and jailed by the police. The leaders were also tired. "Hang on a little bit longer," they told the people.

In April 1956, the Dallas Transit Company announced it was ending segregation on its buses.

King was inside a courtroom, fighting one of the seemingly endless charges against the MIA, when a note was passed to him. He opened it and read,

> The United States Supreme Court today affirmed a decision of a special three-judge U.S. District Court in declaring Alabama's state and local laws requiring segregation on buses unconstitutional.

The Supreme Court had held that segregation on public buses was illegal! The MIA had won. Suddenly, King felt very tired. The long battle in Montgomery was over, but for Martin Luther King, Jr., and his family, it was just the beginning of a much harder and higher climb.

Reverend Martin Luther King, Jr. was arrested for loitering in 1958.

MARTIN LUTHER KING, JR.

After the success of the bus boycott in Montgomery, Martin Luther King, Jr., became the leader of the nonviolent approach to social change. Dr. King met with President Eisenhower and Vice-President Richard Nixon and attended the independence ceremonies of Ghana in Africa. In early January 1957, Dr. King met with southern black ministers to form the Southern Christian Leadership Conference (SCLC). King was elected the first president, and Ralph Abernathy was elected the treasurer. The main office was located in Atlanta, Georgia. Their purpose was to work toward advancing the cause of freedom and justice in America through nonviolent protests.

The first thing that King did as leader of the SCLC was to contact and coordinate his efforts with other civil rights organizations. Along with Roy Wilkins of the NAACP and A. Philip Randolph, King helped plan a march on Washington to emphasize the need for more civil rights legislation. On May 17, 1957, nearly twenty-five thousand people attended the first mass rally. King spoke to the audience in his rich baritone voice, saying, "Give us the ballot and we won't have to worry the federal government" about our basic rights.

In 1958 King wrote his first book, *Stride Toward Freedom*; he survived an assassination attempt and visited India, home of Mahatma Gandhi, the man who had helped free India by using nonviolence, or passive resistance. King greatly admired Gandhi and his work.

THE MOVEMENT

In November 1960 John Fitzgerald Kennedy won a very close election against Richard Nixon. Besides being the youngest president ever elected, Kennedy was also the first Roman Catholic to hold the highest office in the country. He represented fresh, youthful ideas. His inaugural speech inspired young people to become active in their country, and from every corner of the United States they answered his call to serve. It was American youths who brought the civil rights issue to the forefront and launched an era known as the Movement. The Movement included sit-ins, voter registration, boycotts, and peaceful demonstrations.

John F. Kennedy named his brother Robert to the post of attorney general. Robert Kennedy would make a big difference in the civil rights movement. Thirty-five-year-old Robert Kennedy

President John F. Kennedy and his brother, Attorney General Robert F. Kennedy

had earned the nickname ''Ruthless Bobby'' because of fierce political battles he had fought and won. Yet there are those who say that he was an intensely compassionate and sensitive man. Like most human beings, he was perhaps a bit of both. But one thing is sure—Bobby Kennedy was not one to back down in a fight, as those who opposed him would soon learn. For the first time in many years, blacks and other minorities had an active supporter of civil rights in Bobby Kennedy.

*Pickets outside a
Woolworth store in
Harlem, New York*

The Sit-ins

Young blacks wanted to be a part of Kennedy's "New Frontier," but throughout the South there were constant reminders that there were two societies, one for whites and one for blacks. There were the "For Whites Only" signs, the separate drinking fountains, the Jim Crow section in the movies, the continued segregation of schools in spite of the *Brown* decision, and high unemployment. The older generation of blacks kept saying that things were getting better, that things were changing. But the younger generation was growing restless and had very little patience.

Joseph McNeill, a freshman at North Carolina Agricultural and Technical College in Greensboro, North Carolina, was refused service at the bus terminal lunch counter. He was still very upset when he told his friends and roommates—Franklin McCain, Ezell Blair, and David Richmond—about the incident. The young men stayed up late to discuss the situation. Finally, it was decided that they had talked long enough. Now it was time to do something.

The plan called for direct action. They would sit at a segregated lunch counter until they were served. According to the plan, the four freshmen went to the local Woolworth store. They bought a few school supplies, then sat at the lunch counter. The waitress said they did not serve Negroes.

"Yes, you do," came the unexpected response. The students showed their receipts, pointed out that the store did do business with blacks. Why, then, could they not be served at the lunch counter?

The waitress hurried to get help. The white manager asked the students to leave. They refused and remained seated until the store closed.

That evening, fifty students gathered in a dormitory room and formed the Student Executive Committee for Justice. They voted to continue the sit-in. The rules were simple: dress neatly, look straight ahead, do not budge no matter what, and never resort to violence. The group was committed to the nonviolent protests that Martin Luther King, Jr., had used successfully in Montgomery.

Several days later, four black women sat with McCain and McNeill. Two days later they were joined by three white students from a nearby woman's college. Over three hundred young students, black and white, demonstrated on Friday, February 5, 1960, followed by a mass rally with over sixteen hundred participants. It was a modern-day first; they were being called the New Abolitionists. Their goal was to end segregation.

Angered by it all, the white power structure refused to negotiate in good faith. The students called for and received adult support. All the downtown stores were boycotted, and profits dwindled. No matter how many sales they ran, nothing could get the black community to shop. When they were on the verge of financial

Sit-in demonstrators in Woolworth's main store in downtown Atlanta

collapse, the store owners relented, and lunch counters were desegregated in Greensboro, North Carolina. On that day in July 1960, when a white and black student sat side by side at the counter and ordered coffee and doughnuts, the world did not end.

The Greensboro students set an example by showing what could be done elsewhere. In cities all over the South, young college students led demonstrations, boycotts, and sit-ins.

In Atlanta, Julian Bond, a student at Morehouse College, and his friend Lonnie King became nonviolent student leaders. On March 9, 1960, a full-page advertisement appeared in the Atlanta *Constitution*, the *Journal*, and the *Daily Word* that was titled "An Appeal to Civil Rights." Essentially, it supported the students in Greensboro and then called for action in Atlanta: "Today's youth will not sit by submissively, while being denied all the rights, privileges, and joys of life." In the document the students demanded an immediate end to segregation as well as fair housing, equal job opportunities, better health-care facilities, and voting rights. The Atlanta students followed up with sit-ins at movies, lunch counters, and department stores.

Julian Bond

Sit-in Rules

In Nashville, Tennessee, students decided to support the Greensboro students by also conducting sit-ins and boycotts. James Lawson, a theology student at Vanderbilt University, and Marion Barry and Diane Nash from Fisk University were the principal leaders.

Lawson drew up rules for the Nashville sit-ins that were later applied to all nonviolent protests:

"Don't strike back if cursed or abused.

Don't laugh out.

Don't hold conversations with your fellow workers.

Don't leave your seats until your leader has given you instructions to do so.

Don't block entrances to the stores and the aisles.

Show yourself courteous and friendly at all times.

Sit straight and always face the counter.

Report all serious incidents to your leader.

Refer all information to your leader in a polite manner.

Remember love and nonviolence.

May God bless each of you."

One student described what it was like to be in the sit-ins:

> Young kids threw french fried potatoes at us, and gum, and cigarette
> butts. . . The policemen simply lined up behind us and peeled us two
> by two off the stools. . . . The crowd in the store . . . shouted out
> approval. . . . Three paddy wagons were blinking at us from the street.
> Once more we had to walk through those crowds. Someone spit right
> in front of me. . . . The TV cameras took lots of pictures and we drove
> off to the Nashville city jail.

The students read Martin Luther King's book *Stride Towards
Freedom* and gained courage:

> Once plagued with a tragic sense of inferiority resulting from the
> crippling effects of slavery and segregation, the Negro has now been
> driven to reevaluate himself. He has come to feel that he is somebody.
> His religion reveals to him that God loves all His children and that the
> important thing about a man is . . . not the texture of his hair or the
> color of his skin but his eternal worth to God. . . . There is a new
> Negro in the South, with a new sense of dignity and destiny.

In October the Student Nonviolent Coordinating Committee
(SNCC, pronounced "snick") was formed as a permanent
organization. Marion Barry was the first chairperson. The goals of
SNCC were the same as those set by Douglass, DuBois, Trotter,
Randolph, and King: "to speed up school desegregation, to enact
fair employment laws, to ensure the right to vote."

Membership in SNCC was open to all those who believed in the
goals of the Movement. And young people all over America
joined by the hundreds—the thousands. The budget of SNCC was
a scant $14,000 but few were worried about money. The workers
were funded with high ideals and bolstered by the courage they
gathered from their unity of thought and their oneness of
purpose. Young people who could have been having a good time
elsewhere chose to make a difference by putting their bodies on

Felton Turner told authorities that four armed, masked white men abducted him, took him to a wooded area, beat him, and carved the Klan letters on him, before leaving him hanging upsidedown in a tree.

the line for what they believed in. In return they got yelled at, beaten, jailed, and killed. Once committed, though, not many turned back. The nation was standing on the threshold of President Kennedy's New Frontier, and it was scary. Within the year, over fifty thousand people had demonstrated against segregation in some way. One elderly woman sent twenty-five cents to SNCC and a note saying that it was all she could spare. She wanted to give some kind of support to the Movement.

As the sit-in protests spread throughout the South, so did the violence. In Orangeburg, South Carolina, over one thousand black and white students were arrested. In Montgomery, Governor John M. Patterson insisted that thirty-five students who had been involved in a sit-in at the courthouse snack shop be expelled from school. Students demonstrated in protest and threatened to boycott the school if the thirty-five students were dismissed.

In Atlanta, acid was thrown in a sit-in leader's face. In Frankfort, Kentucky, a black gymnasium was burned; in Columbia, South Carolina, a student was stabbed; and in Houston, Texas, a twenty-seven-year-old black man was kidnapped, flogged, and had the symbol "KKK" carved in his abdomen. In

Richard Hatcher (left), mayor of Gary, Indiana, and Marion Barry (right), mayor of Washington, D.C., in 1980

Mississippi, dogs were set on peaceful protesters, and policemen used chains and clubs to break up rallies.

The most common attack made on the young protesters was to imply that they were Communist inspired. The Nashville *Banner* reported, "There is no place in Nashville for flannel-mouthed agitators, white or colored—under whatever sponsorship, imported for preachment of mass disorder; self-supported vagrants, or paid agents of strife-breeding organizations."

In response Marion Barry of SNCC responded eloquently, "Communism seeks power, ignores people, and thrives on social conflict. We seek a community in which man can realize the full meaning of the self which demands open relationship with others."

Whenever asked, the civil rights workers reinforced the concept that their goals were to help preserve the Constitution, not to dismantle it; not to destroy America, but to make it a better place for all its people.

In spite of all the resistance, the sit-ins were working. In some places, managers of integrated facilities were saying publicly that it was not all that bad. There was much more involved than a hamburger and french fries.

James Farmer, leader of CORE, sits with a group of demonstrators on Atlantic City's Boardwalk. They were seeking support for an almost all-black group of delegates from Mississippi.

The Congress of Racial Equality (CORE)

A group that also joined in the struggle for civil rights was the Congress of Racial Equality (CORE). In 1961 James Farmer became the national director. Farmer received his B.A. degree in chemistry from Wiley College in Marshall, Texas, when he was eighteen years old. He studied for the ministry at Howard University in Washington, D.C., but was never ordained. "I didn't see how I could honestly preach the Gospel of Christ in a church that practiced discrimination," he said. "But I never abandoned His teaching. It is still very much part of my thinking."

In 1942 Farmer and several students at the University of Chicago organized the first chapter of CORE. In 1961 Farmer contacted Martin Luther King, Jr., and told him that CORE, in conjunction with SNCC, was going to begin a series of "freedom rides." Farmer knew that in 1946 the Supreme Court had outlawed segregation on interstate bus and train travel and in 1960 had extended the ban to terminals as well. For the most part, southern terminals and bus stations remained segregated. The riders would call attention to the practice and perhaps bring about change.

Outside of Anniston, Alabama, the freedom riders bus was set afire. The passengers escaped injury, but the bus was destroyed.

Farmer informed all authorities about his plans. On May 1, 1961, seven blacks and six whites met in Washington, D.C., to learn nonviolent techniques. The trip began on May 4, 1961, in Washington and was supposed to go to New Orleans. The group boarded two buses, a Trailways and a Greyhound. The trip ran smoothly until May 14, 1961 (Mother's Day). The Greyhound bus was stopped just outside Anniston, Alabama. The tires were flattened, and the bus was burned. The freedom riders refused to be stopped. They took another bus into Birmingham. Meanwhile, an hour outside Anniston, the Trailways bus was boarded by eight hoodlums. They beat the black riders with planks and chains. When James Peck and Walter Berman, the two whites aboard, tried to help, they were also beaten. After the beating, Peck had to have fifty stitches in his head.

A group of freedom riders arrested in Jackson, Mississippi

Martin Luther King tried to get the students to stop, to turn back, but they refused. Attorney General Robert Kennedy was being informed of what was happening every mile of the way. He also called for the freedom rides to stop before someone was seriously hurt. The students defiantly asked, Why? Was it not the right of a citizen to ride a bus? They had done nothing wrong, yet somehow they were being blamed for the violence against them. One student said that it was like a man being shot and then having the murderer blame him for dying.

That point was made clearer when John Siegenthaler, who was sent by President John F. Kennedy to Montgomery as an observer, was struck and left unconscious in the middle of the street by an angry mob. The mob had just attacked one of the freedom buses. Reporters were victimized, and their equipment was smashed. It was chaos.

When Robert Kennedy called Governor Patterson, he was told that the governor was out and could not be located. Kennedy wasted no more time. He had the Justice Department attorneys go into federal district court in Montgomery to enjoin anyone who was interfering with peaceful interstate travel; he sent the FBI to investigate the violence connected with the freedom rides; and he sent U.S. marshals to protect the riders.

Robert Kennedy asked Martin Luther King to call off the freedom rides. Kennedy said that he could not guarantee the riders' safety and that someone was bound to get hurt. Besides, President Kennedy was in Vienna meeting with Soviet Premier Nikita Khrushchev. He said that the news coverage was embarrassing.

King also believed that the freedom rides were too dangerous and not worth the risk. But SNCC and CORE did not agree with Kennedy or King. The rides continued into the summer. Finally, at Robert Kennedy's request, the Interstate Commerce Commission issued regulations that ended segregated facilities in interstate bus stations that were to take effect on November 1, 1961. It would be two years later before systematic segregation of blacks in interstate transportation would disappear.

Voter Registration

Membership in CORE, the NAACP, and SNCC increased. Financial support for these organizations began coming in from all over the world, along with encouraging letters. The rule of the day was nonviolence, to meet violence with "soul force." But support for white citizens' councils, neo-Nazi groups, and the Ku Klux Klan also grew. Their response to nonviolence was predictable—crush with brute force.

In October 1963, a record number of registered blacks turned out to vote in Cambridge, Maryland.

It was decided by SNCC to work on voter registration. The target was Mississippi, where blacks made up a large percentage of the population but where less than 1 percent were registered voters.

The early SNCC voter registration workers were beaten, their headquarters and homes were burned, and in many cases they were jailed. They endured it all nonviolently. But it was the murder of Herbert Lee that intensified the situation. Lee, a poor Mississippi farmer, was on his way to register and was killed.

According to Robert Moses, who was the SNCC field coordinator in McComb County, this is what happened: "Herbert Lee, a Negro farmer, was killed in Amite County.... Lee's body lay on the ground that morning for two hours, uncovered, until they finally got a funeral home in McComb to take it in. No one in Liberty would touch it."

In the McComb newspaper the next day, there was a short article that stated that Herbert Lee was shot because he had attacked a white man. There were no witnesses who would come forward to testify, so Lee's murderer was not convicted. Moses responded emotionally, "[One] might have thought he'd [Lee] been a bum. There was no mention that Lee was a farmer, that he had a family, nine kids, beautiful kids, and that he had farmed all his life in Amite County." And all Herbert Lee wanted to do was register to vote.

A NEW ATTITUDE

During that summer, whites and blacks sat side by side in damp, dark jail cells, sharing tears and a song: "We Shall Overcome." One white SNCC worker received a letter from his girl, asking why he would leave the comfort of his upper-class home (heaven) to help fight for Negro freedom. This is an excerpt from the young man's response:

> I do not understand.... It's no heaven on earth I left.... Depends on what you mean by heaven. If you mean a place where everyone has so much money they have no sensitivity—no love, no sympathy, and no hopes beyond their own narrow little worlds.... But to me the conceited, loud, self-centered, All-American free white and twenty-one college boy stinks.... If I did not have my friends, I would be very much alone. And I don't want to eat in anyone's restaurant alone, to go to nobody's movie alone, to swim in nobody's pool alone. You dig?

The letter reflects the spirit of the day, a new attitude that was

Dashikis, African jewelry, and Afro hairstyles were outward manifestations of the black is beautiful movement.

taking shape among whites. Pride was growing also among blacks. Beauty was being seen from a different perspective. Parents began teaching their children that they were black and very beautiful. A new hairstyle called the "Afro" was being worn. The hair was worn naturally and without shame. Even terms were changing. "Black" became preferable to "colored."

BIRMINGHAM

In January 1963 Martin Luther King announced that SCLC was going to Birmingham to work with the Reverend Fred Shuttlesworth, a civil rights leader in Birmingham. The goal was to integrate public facilities and department stores.

George Wallace was the newly elected governor of Alabama. He had won by saying that there would be no integration in Alabama—*ever*! Eugene "Bull" Connor, the police commissioner, promised that the streets would run red with blood if there were any attempts to integrate the city of Birmingham.

King and Abernathy arrived in Birmingham and met with leaders in early April. The SCLC strategy was the same—peaceful marches, boycotts, and sit-ins.

217

Police dogs were used to break up demonstrations in Birmingham, Alabama in May 1963.

On Wednesday, April 10, Martin Luther King and other leaders were given a court injunction that ordered them not to march. King and Abernathy defied the order and led the march on Good Friday. They were promptly arrested.

Eight Alabama clergymen issued a public statement that criticized the civil rights movement and Dr. King's leadership. They wrote, "We recognize the natural impatience of people who feel that their hopes are slow in being realized. But we are convinced that these demonstrations are unwise and untimely."

From his jail cell, with a single light swinging overhead, King wrote a response to his fellow clergymen. It is appropriately entitled "Letter from Birmingham Jail" and has become a classic in protest literature. King illustrates why black Americans were not willing to wait.

We have waited for more than 340 years for our constitutional and God-given rights. The nations of Asia and Africa are moving with jetlike speed toward gaining political independence, but we still creep at horse-and-buggy pace toward gaining a cup of coffee at a lunch counter. Perhaps it is easy for those who have never felt the stinging darts of segregation to say, "Wait." But when you have seen vicious mobs lynch your mothers and fathers at will and drown your sisters and brothers at whim; when you have seen hate-filled policemen curse, kick and even kill your black brothers and sisters; when you see the vast majority of your twenty million Negro brothers smothering in an airtight cage of poverty in the midst of an affluent society . . . then you will understand why we find it difficult to wait.

Dr. King was criticized because, when he led the protest demonstrators, he was technically breaking the law. Dr. King responded,

You express a great deal of anxiety over our willingness to break laws. This is certainly a legitimate concern. Since we so diligently urge people to obey the Supreme Court's decision of 1954 outlawing segregation in the public schools, at first glance it may seem rather paradoxical for us consciously to break laws. One may well ask: "How can you advocate breaking some laws and obeying others?" The answer lies in the fact that there are two types of laws; just and unjust. I would be the first to advocate obeying just laws. One has not only a legal but a moral responsibility to obey just laws. Conversely, one has a moral responsibility to disobey unjust laws. I would agree with St. Augustine that "an unjust law is no law at all."

King and Abernathy were released from jail on April 20, 1963. Meanwhile, a march had been planned for May 2. Almost one thousand people gathered at the Sixteenth Street Baptist Church, where the Reverend Shuttlesworth was the pastor. Dr. King spoke to the group, then two by two they began the march. Less than a block away, Bull Connor, the police commissioner, waited. "Arrest them all," he shouted. Nine hundred youths were brutally arrested that day.

The next day twenty-five thousand people turned out. This time, adults were with their children. As the marchers turned the corner, holding hands and singing, Bull Connor ordered them to turn around. They refused and kept marching. An order was given, and huge fire hoses sprayed water into the crowd. The force of the water was powerful enough to strip bark off nearby trees. People were dashed against buildings and cars. In the midst of all the confusion and pain, attack dogs were released on fleeing demonstrators—and the country watched it all on the television news.

On May 5 a group of three thousand people staged a protest march, and Connor was ready for them. "Turn back," he ordered. The marchers pressed forward saying they would not turn away until justice was served. As they advanced, Bull Connor ordered the hoses turned on, but something wonderful happened. The firemen refused to obey an "unjust order." Policemen, many with tears in their eyes, parted and let the marchers through.

Protests continued all week, and arrests continued. The protesters would not stop coming; they would not stop asking for their rights. Birmingham businessmen, who by this time were facing financial ruin, forced local politicians to negotiate a settlement. It was agreed that rest rooms, lunch counters, fitting rooms, and drinking fountains would be desegregated within ninety days. Employment opportunities also would be opened to blacks.

Once the word got out that an agreement had been made, Birmingham exploded into violence. White-supremacy groups retaliated by bombing houses, churches, cars, and black businesses. So many homes were bombed in one area that it was renamed "Dynamite Hill."

The violence continued. Medgar Evers, a civil rights leader in

Medgar Evers, Mississippi field secretary for the NAACP, was shot and killed as he left his car after returning to his home from an integration rally.

Mississippi, was killed in front of his home by hate-filled white extremists. It was a season of suffering—but it had only just begun.

President Kennedy Responds

President John F. Kennedy could not ride the middle road on civil rights any longer. The time had come when he had to take a position. Robert Kennedy encouraged the president to take a firm stand on the civil rights issue. President Kennedy listened to all his advisors, then made up his own mind. He decided to give his full support to the movement. On June 11, 1963, he appealed to the nation, making one of the strongest statements that any twentieth-century president had made on behalf of civil rights:

> It ought to be possible, therefore, for American students of any color to attend any public institution they select without having to be backed up by troops. It ought to be possible for American consumers of any color to receive equal service in places of public accommodation, such as hotels and restaurants, and theatres and retail stores, without being forced to resort to demonstrations in the street.

President Kennedy felt that the situation occurring in the South was a "moral crisis" that could not be quieted by token moves and talk: "It is a time to act in the Congress." And he backed up his words with action.

THE MARCH ON WASHINGTON

With the Kennedy administration giving support, the movement grew stronger and bolder. Not since Reconstruction had such a giant step been made in so short a time. Black leaders planned another march on Washington to coincide with the one-hundredth anniversary of the Emancipation Proclamation, which had been signed in 1863. They planned to highlight the fact that one hundred years had passed and black people still were not free in America.

On August 28, 1963, nearly 250,000 black and white people assembled on the grounds of the Lincoln Memorial in

Before the March on Washington, prominent people interested in the march and civil rights met with President John F. Kennedy in the White House. Dr. Martin Luther King, from the Christian Leadership Conference, is fourth from the left, and Roy Wilkins, from the NAACP, is on the right.

Washington, D.C., to express their concern about a problem that affected the entire United States, an issue that had been ignored too long. Civil rights legislation had been sent to Congress, and they wanted to pressure Congress into passing it without a lot of lengthy debates and filibusters. Southerners used filibusters to prevent action on several important pieces of civil rights legislation.

A host of guests and speakers addressed the crowd. Then the elderly A. Philip Randolph introduced Martin Luther King, Jr., as "the moral leader of the nation." The crowd thundered with applause.

Of all that was said on that day, King's "I Have a Dream" speech is the most remembered. The beauty of the speech is in its simplicity; the power of the speech was in the delivery; the greatness of the speech is in its message. Martin Luther King was a stirring orator, one who, according to a classmate, could mesmerize an audience merely by reciting the alphabet.

Reverend Martin Luther King, Jr., delivers his famous "I Have a Dream" speech. He said the march was the "greatest demonstration of freedom in the history of our nation."

On the day of the march, Dr. King stepped to the podium and delivered a flawless oration without a note in front of him:

> There are those who are asking the devotees of civil rights, "when will you be satisfied?" We can never be satisfied as long as the Negro is the victim of the unspeakable horrors of police brutality. We can never be satisfied as long as our bodies, heavy with the fatigue of travel, cannot gain lodging in the motels of the highways and the hotels of the cities. We cannot be satisfied as long as the Negro's basic mobility is from a smaller ghetto to a larger one. We can never be satisfied as long as a Negro in Mississippi cannot vote and a Negro in New York believes he has nothing for which to vote.

People shouted "Amen, Amen." Some held hands and swayed back and forth. King continued:

> I have a dream today. I have a dream that one day the state of Alabama, whose governor's lips are presently dripping with the words of interposition and nullification, will be transformed into a situation where little black boys and black girls will be able to join hands with little white boys and white girls and walk together as sisters and brothers. I have a dream today.

Each time that King revealed a vision from his dream, the crowd cried out for him to continue. People held hands, hugged each other, and wept openly. It was a moving, highly charged moment in American history. King's powerful address kept building higher and higher. He ended with:

> When we let freedom ring, when we let it ring from every village and every hamlet, from every state and every city, we will be able to speed up that day when all of God's children, black men and white men, Jews and Gentiles, Protestants and Catholics, will be able to join hands and sing in the words of the old Negro spiritual, "Free at last! free at last! thank God almighty, we are free at last!"

And the crowd roared its approval. It is ironic that on the day that

Dr. King delivered his speech, W.E.B. DuBois died in Ghana at the age of ninety-five.

Afterward, the members of the march committee were greeted by President Kennedy at the White House. Roy Wilkins described the president as being delighted with the success of the event. He also was relieved that violence had not marred the day.

All was not as unified as it appeared on the surface. Within the movement there were rumblings of discontent. John Lewis, chairman of SNCC, had been forced to tone down his speech because it was considered too militant. James Farmer of CORE did not attend the march. He remained in a Louisiana jail cell, saying that the message of the march was not strong enough. Malcolm X, a radical black Muslim minister, called it the "Farce on Washington."

But regardless of the varying opinions, the march on Washington was a huge success. In the history of human rights, the march of 1963 is an unforgettable event.

A SEASON OF SADNESS

The Birmingham Church Bombing

Not all the memorable events in the civil rights struggle were as pleasant and inspiring as was the march on Washington. Another unforgettable moment was the Birmingham church bombing.

Bitterness and hatred are emotions that lead people to do terrible things. On September 15, 1963, a bomb was hurled into the Sixteenth Avenue Baptist Church in Birmingham, Alabama. Four black girls who had arrived to attend Sunday school were killed. King rushed to Birmingham. "How high is the price for freedom?" he asked.

Firemen and ambulance attendants remove a body from the wreckage of the Sixteenth Avenue Baptist Church in Birmingham.

The bombing and other cowardly acts of a few desperate men inadvertently made allies of people who ordinarily would not have been. Southerners were slowly becoming fed up with the senseless violence. They began speaking out. The day after the bombing, on September 15, 1963, a young white lawyer named Charles Morgan, Jr., spoke to the Young Men's Business Club. This is an excerpt from what Morgan said:

> Four little girls were killed in Birmingham Sunday. A mad, remorseful, worried community asks "Who did it? Who threw that bomb? Was it a Negro or a white?" . . . Who is guilty? A moderate mayor elected to change things in Birmingham and who moves so slowly and looks elsewhere for leadership? A business community which shrugs its shoulders and looks to the police or perhaps somewhere else for leadership? A newspaper which has tried so hard of late, yet finds it necessary to lecture Negroes every time a Negro home is bombed? A Governor who offers a reward but mentions not his own failure to preserve either segregation or law and order? And what of those lawyers and politicians who counsel people as to what the law is not when they know full well what the law is? Those four little Negro girls were human beings.

For expressing his opinion, Morgan was harassed to the point where he had to leave Birmingham. But others who thought like him were speaking out more.

Kennedy Is Assassinated

In Dallas, Texas, on November 22, 1963, President John F. Kennedy was shot at 12:30 P.M. by Lee Harvey Oswald. Once again the country mourned the death of its president. The loss of Kennedy was particularly difficult. He was so young and so full of energy. For civil rights workers it was shattering. Immediately, people started to ask, "What's going to happen now?"

Lyndon B. Johnson was sworn in as president at 2:30 P.M. on November 22. Two days later, Oswald was taken into custody, but, as he was being transferred from one place to another, Oswald was shot by Jack Ruby, a Dallas nightclub owner.

The funeral procession of President John Fitzgerald Kennedy

The nation was literally paralyzed with shock, grief, and a terrible sense of loss. When would it end? People were convinced that it was a conspiracy. But on September 24, 1964, the Warren Commission released the report of its investigation. The 296,000-word report stated that there was "no conspiracy, domestic or foreign."

Lyndon B. Johnson Becomes President

Lyndon Johnson was a southern Democrat with years of political experience in the Senate. Blacks were concerned about whether he was going to be an ally or an enemy. The irony is that this southerner became the best friend that the civil rights movement ever had.

On November 27, 1963, Johnson addressed Congress and assured the world and the American people that he would carry out Kennedy's policies. At the beginning of the year, Johnson presented his program that was designed to wage "war on poverty."

In early 1964 not too many Americans were aware of or

President Lyndon Johnson uses several pens as he signs into law the "War on Poverty" Bill.

concerned about the small, Southeast Asian country of Vietnam. Soon, though, they would be. In August 1964 Congress passed the Gulf of Tonkin Resolution. President Johnson was given the power "to take necessary measures to repel any army attack against the forces of the United States and to prevent further aggression." Thereafter, Vietnam moved from the fifth page of the newspaper to the front page. But even then, small numbers of people were exercising their right to speak out against U.S. intervention in Southeast Asia.

Freedom Summer

In the summer of 1964, SNCC, CORE, and the SCLC sponsored a voter registration drive. They knew from the work that had been done previously that it was not going to be an easy task. In June two white CORE workers, Andrew Goodman and Michael Schwerner, traveled to Mississippi. They were met and shown around by James Chaney. Just outside Philadelphia, Mississippi, their car was pulled over by local deputies. The three civil rights workers were never seen alive again. Their bodies were found in August in a mud dam in the Tallahaga River. Freedom is costly!

That same summer President Lyndon Johnson signed the Civil Rights Bill. It was stronger and broader than the one recommended by John F. Kennedy. Senator Hubert Humphrey from Minnesota and Senator Everett Dirksen from Illinois were credited with pushing it through. It was not surprising that Humphrey, a long-time civil rights advocate, had worked so hard to pass the bill. But Dirksen was not noted for supporting civil rights legislation. When asked why he had supported it, he quoted Victor Hugo: "No army can withstand the strength of an idea whose time has come."

Reverend Martin Luther King, Jr., receives the Nobel Peace Prize in Oslo, Norway. He was cited for his nonviolent leadership of the American civil rights movement.

The Time Has Come

Twenty-one white men—most of them members of the Ku Klux Klan—including a local sheriff and his deputy, were arrested for the murder of the three slain civil rights workers on December 4, 1964. That same day Martin Luther King left for Norway to accept his Nobel Peace Prize. Maybe, people began to think, the time for peace and justice had finally come.

King informed the press that all his $54,000 prize money was going to the various civil rights organizations. He was more convinced than ever that violence accomplished nothing. "I refuse to accept the view that mankind is so tragically bound to the starless midnight of racism and war that the bright daylight of peace and brotherhood can never become a reality. . . . There is still hope for a brighter tomorrow."

MALCOLM X

There were those who did not agree with the nonviolent approach to bring about change. Not all black leaders shared King's dreams of brotherhood or believed that integration was the solution to the black man's problems. Malcolm X was the most radical of King's opponents, a minister in the Black Muslim Movement, which was headquartered in Chicago, Illinois.

Malcolm X was born Malcolm Little. At age four, his house was burned by the Ku Klux Klan. His father was a follower of Marcus Garvey and died under mysterious circumstances when Malcolm was six years old. As a young teenager, Malcolm was sent to Boston, where he dropped out of school and began a life of street crime. Eventually, he ended up in prison. While in prison, Malcolm became interested in the Black Muslim religion that was headed by Elijah Muhammad. Muslim rules were strict and forbade the use of drugs, tobacco, narcotics, or alcohol. Muslims encouraged education, with emphasis on black culture, racial pride, and family unity.

Malcolm also began his education in prison by reading volumes of books on every subject, including the dictionary and a set of encyclopedias. After his release from prison, he joined the Muslims, and, according to the custom, he changed his name to Malcolm X. For years Malcolm served as a Muslim minister and edited their newspaper, *Muhammad Speaks*. However, in November 1963, Malcolm split from Elijah Muhammad's group and formed his own sect.

Martin Luther King's followers were mostly well-educated southern blacks with middle-class backgrounds. Malcolm's followers were undereducated and underemployed northern ghetto dwellers. Malcolm's people had a different set of problems

Malcolm X encouraged blacks to help each other to raise their economic power.

than the sharecroppers in Mississippi had. A southern black man could not eat at a Mississippi lunch counter. A northern black could eat anywhere he wanted, but he did not have the money because he did not have a job. Malcolm X spoke to the needs of people who lived in rat-infested tenements. Malcolm X spoke to people who were chronically unemployed and strung out on drugs. Malcolm X spoke in terms that people without hope could understand — he had been there.

As the spokesman for black nationalism, Malcolm argued that integration was not what black people needed — they needed economic power. He encouraged blacks to start their own businesses, to patronize each other's businesses, and to build

Blacks on a Harlem, New York, street

financial and educational institutions that helped black people help themselves. "The cornerstones of this country's operation are economic and political strength and power," he said. "The black man doesn't have the economic strength—and it will take time for him to build it. But right now the American black man has the political strength and power to change his destiny overnight."

He asked audiences all over the country how many black people controlled enormous amounts of wealth or sat on corporate boards of directors. Not many. "Why not?" he often probed. "Racism!" Malcolm suggested—the *same* racism that kept black children from going to all-white schools in the South also kept black men from becoming managers, supervisors, presidents, and board members of all-white northern corporations. In 1964 such thoughts were considered absurd, if not altogether mad.

Malcolm did not seem to care much what people thought of him or his ideas. It was "standing room only" every time he spoke, so people were definitely listening.

His opposition to the nonviolent movement was based on his belief that it benefited no one to submit to a beating if the situation remained the same. "What good is it?" he asked. He advised blacks to stop asking whites to "give" them their rights. Civil rights were already theirs; they had earned them by giving America "four hundred years of toil."

He would ask large audiences what they would do if someone had something that was rightfully theirs. Would they ask for it politely? But if they couldn't get it, then what would they do? They would take it, wouldn't they? He got thunderous applause.

Malcolm was a militant, a black nationalist, and an advocate of black racial pride and dignity. He used words such as "revolution," which frightened people in 1964. In 1964 his ideas were frightening to both blacks and whites, and they still are.

He felt that blacks have the same rights as whites. These are the rights that George Washington fought for:

"We are fighting for recognition as human beings. We are fighting for the right to live as free humans in this society. In fact, we are actually fighting for rights that are even greater than civil rights and that is human rights.

"We must have human rights before we can secure civil rights. We must be respected as humans before we can be recognized as citizens."

Malcolm offered black people another point of view in the

struggle for civil rights in America. Some agreed with his philosophy, but a majority of blacks did not support his ideas in 1964.

Once Malcolm X broke with the Nation of Islam, he founded the Muslim Mosque, Incorporated, in New York City. In 1964 Malcolm X visited Mecca in Saudi Arabia, Ghana, and other African countries. He spoke with government officials, diplomats, and leaders. Returning to the United States, Malcolm began showing a slight shift in his attitude. The problems of black Americans, he believed, were linked to those of yellow, brown, black, and red people everywhere. His attitude toward the white race had changed slightly. "If you attack him because he is white, you give him no out. He can't stop being white. We've got to give the man a chance."

America would never know the events that would have taken place had Malcolm been allowed to stay in the civil rights struggle. He was assassinated in 1965 by members of Elijah Muhammad's Muslim sect. His voice was silent but not his ideas.

PRESIDENT JOHNSON WINS

On November 3, 1964, Lyndon B. Johnson and Hubert Humphrey, presidential and vice-presidential candidates, respectively, won with a large percentage of the votes. Labor, liberals, and blacks united to vote for the Democratic ticket. Six million blacks voted—two million more than had voted in 1960— and 94 percent of them voted for Johnson rather than Barry M. Goldwater, the Republican candidate. Civil rights remained a key political issue, but students at the University of California held a rally where they spoke out against the "undeclared" war in Vietnam. It was a prelude to what was yet to come.

Jeannette Rankin, first woman member of Congress, leads several thousand women on a march from Union Station to the Capitol in Washington, D.C. to protest the war in Vietnam. Miss Rankin is in the center, wearing glasses.

TIME LINE 1965–Present

1965 Lyndon B. Johnson and Hubert H. Humphrey sworn in as president and vice-president; Black Muslims assassinate Malcolm X in New York; Selma to Montgomery protest march; Voting Rights Act signed by President Johnson; Race riot in Watts district of Los Angeles

1966 *Miranda v. Arizona*, Supreme Court rules that an accused person must be told his/her rights before being held or questioned by police authorities; Major rioting in northern cities; Demonstrations against American involvement in Vietnam; Edward Brooke, Republican, is first black senator from Massachusetts (reelected in 1972)

1967 Thurgood Marshall, great-grandson of a slave, becomes the first black Supreme Court Justice; Carl Stokes and Richard Hatcher are first blacks elected mayors in large, northern cities; Blacks elected to legislative positions in Georgia, Mississippi, and Virginia

1968 Martin Luther King, Jr., assassinated by James Earl Ray in Memphis, Tennessee; Robert F. Kennedy assassinated by Sirhan Sirhan in California; Shirley Chisholm is first black woman to be elected to House of Representatives; Student militancy against "the Establishment" rises along with a white middle-class backlash

1969 Richard Nixon sworn in as 37th president, and Spiro Agnew as vice-president; Neil Armstrong walks on the moon; Seventy-eight Native Americans seize Alcatraz Island in San Francisco

1970 Four Kent State University students are killed by national guardsmen during anti-Vietman protest; Two black Jackson State College students killed during a demonstration

1971 Supreme Court validates the use of busing to achieve racial balance in public schools

1972   Shirley Chisholm runs for the presidency to highlight concerns of blacks and women; Former Alabama governor, George Wallace, a states' rights candidate, is shot and partially paralyzed while campaigning for the presidency; Richard Nixon receives overwhelming victory over Democratic candidate, George McGovern, but his second term is clouded by "Watergate"

1973   Nearly three hundred members of the American Indian Movement take over Wounded Knee, South Dakota, to protest the ineffectiveness of the Bureau of Indian Affairs; Vice-president Spiro Agnew resigns and Gerald Ford fills the vacancy; Congress passes the War Powers Act, restraining the president from sending troops into foreign countries without approval of Congress; Vietnam War ends and troops removed in stages

1974   Impeachment proceedings begin against President Nixon; Nixon resigns and Gerald Ford becomes president; President Ford pardons Nixon of all involvement in the Watergate break-in and cover-up; Rioting in Boston and protests throughout the country concerning busing

1975   International Woman's Year; Military academies opened to women

1976   James (Jimmy) Carter, becomes the first southern president since Reconstruction

1977   President Carter appoints two blacks to important positions: Andrew Young, ambassador to the United Nations, and Patricia Harris, secretary of Housing, Education, and Welfare (HEW)

1978   In the *Bakke* case, the US Supreme Court rules that affirmative action with strict racial quotas is illegal

1979   Iranian Muslims, demanding the return of the Shah to face trial, take sixty-six American hostages; Eldridge Cleaver, black militant and author of *Soul On Ice*, returns to US after living in Libya

1980   After an all-white jury acquits four white policemen of killing a black insurance man, blacks riot for three days in Miami; Ronald Reagan, a Republican conservative, defeats Jimmy Carter to become the 40th president

1981   President Reagan shot by John Hinckley, Jr.; Sandra Day O'Connor becomes the first woman member of the Supreme Court

1982   Equal Rights Amendment defeated

1983   President Reagan supports prayer in school, busing, and decreased federal spending, including many social programs created in the 1960s

1984   Jesse Jackson seeks Democratic presidential nomination; Geraldine Ferraro is the first woman to run for vice-president, on Democratic ticket; More blacks, women, Hispanics, and Asians than ever before elected to national, state, and local positions

1985   Clarence Pendleton, a Reagan appointee to the Civil Rights Commission, speaks out against affirmative action and other protective civil rights safeguards; Jesse Jackson, the most well-known black leader in US, disagrees with Pendleton's position; Bilingual education under attack

1986   Martin Luther King, Jr.'s birthday celebrated as a federal holiday; Racism is expressed more openly and membership in the Ku Klux Klan and neo-Nazis increases; Gramm-Rudman budget cuts affect social programs; John Lewis defeats Julian Bond, both former civil rights workers and members of SNCC, in race for representative from Georgia; Warren Burger resigns as Chief Justice and is replaced by William Rehnquist; Protests against American business support of South African apartheid system of government; Congress votes sanctions against South Africa

1965-Present

CULTURAL AWARENESS

Not all of the civil rights movement took place in the streets and at lunch counters. Many changes and advances came about after years of working quietly behind the scenes.

Minorities were becoming more aware of themselves and of their potential. In the mid-1960s, black history materials were for the most part inaccurate, insensitive, and inadequate. There were few stories that portrayed the black experience with depth and understanding. Although schools were integrated, curricula and textbooks excluded the contributions of blacks, women, and other minorities. Educators, parents, and students began verbalizing their concerns about the lack of good cultural materials. As logical as it sounded, the concept met with overwhelming resistance by opponents who feared that accommodating a multicultural curriculum would result in lowered academic standards.

Through persistence, school districts were convinced that multicultural education was the best approach and that cultural diversity was a strength, not a liability. Still, little material or training was available for the classroom teacher in 1965. Administrators passed their needs and concerns on to publishers and universities that, in turn, began publishing better materials and making multicultural education courses a part of teacher certification. That process took years, and the efforts continue today.

Media and mass communication were another target of awareness groups. Television had no programs with regular black, Asian, or Hispanic stars. Commercials stereotyped women and excluded minority consumers.

The first television show to feature a regular black female star was "Julia," which starred Diahann Carroll. Carroll's successful sitcom was followed by "I Spy," a dramatic series that featured Bill Cosby. Cosby was the first black man to have a starring role in a television series in which brain was used over brawn. He won several Emmy Awards for his role. In the 1980s, Cosby's award-winning sitcom about a black professional family, "The Cosby Show," became the most popular series on television. Slowly, nonwhite faces began appearing in other television shows and movies "though not as frequently as they appeared in real American life.

Advances were made in legitimate theater, too. Black theater groups moved from experimental to mainstream, and blacks began tentatively to appear in classical roles traditionally reserved for white actors. The idea of casting actors and actresses for their abilities, and not their skin colors, was controversial, and there are still many people who feel that a black Emily in Thornton Wilder's "Our Town" is shockingly miscast.

Efforts continue to stop the exploitation and stereotyping of women and minorities in films, radio, television, theater, magazines, and newspapers. In spite of all the efforts, Asians, Hispanics, and women are still underrepresented and stereotyped in the media. In fact, at the National Association for the Advancement of Colored People's annual Image Awards in 1990, the category of Best Actress was eliminated for the fourth time in twenty-three years because there were so few roles available for African-American actresses!

There were very few blacks and Hispanics on police and fire departments in metropolitan cities in 1965, yet these minorities constituted more than 60 percent of the population of large urban

Into the 1990s, blacks, Hispanics, and other minorities continued to have difficulty obtaining positions on college and university faculties. Enrollments at the graduate level are also declining.

cities. And women military officers could be counted on the fingers of one hand. These situations have improved. Today, police, fire, and military academies recruit minorities and women, but their representation in administrative positions still remains low.

Education has long been seen as the cornerstone for minority advancement. Yet, even here, minority representation in teaching and administrative positions lags far behind expectations. Studies in 1990 estimate that only 3 percent to 5 percent of all U.S. faculty in higher education are minorities, compared with a national minority population that approaches 20 percent. (This study does not include women in its minority figures.) Partly, this is a result of a scarcity of qualified doctoral candidates; from 1982 to 1989, the number of doctorates awarded to blacks fell from 1,042 to 811—just 2 percent of the total number. Hispanics received another 2 percent of doctorates awarded, but their numbers have been rising slightly. Still, the underrepresentation is obvious.

Martin Luther King, Jr., speaks to the media about the civil rights movement.

Positions in business, industry, banking, and government were
opening up for minorities and women beginning in the late 1960s,
but high-ranking corporate positions were reserved for white males.
Changes were taking place, but for far too many people those
changes were too few, too slow, and too late.

SELMA, ALABAMA

Without the right to vote, blacks would remain victims, so there
was heavy concentration of blacks in the voting rights drive. In
Selma, Alabama, there were only 355 blacks registered to vote out
of fifteen thousand who were eligible. Martin Luther King, Jr., and
other civil rights leaders planned a march from Selma to Montgomery
to dramatize the problem. On Monday, February 1, 1965, King
and Ralph Abernathy led over 750 people in a march to the Selma
courthouse. Hundreds of marchers were arrested and jailed. The
protests continued, however, and within days the jails were packed.

King announced that there would be a march from Selma to
Montgomery beginning on March 7. Alabama's governor said that
the protest march could not—must not—take place. When it did,
Governor George Wallace made good his threats. Two hundred
state troopers blocked the marchers on the highway. Officers attacked

Black youngsters sing freedom songs in front of the Dallas County Courthouse in Selma, Alabama. The white-helmeted men are sheriff deputies who arrested the group just after this photo was taken.

the group with cattle prods and whips and used horses to disperse the marchers, who offered no resistance.

Then, on March 11, Reverend James Reeb, a Unitarian minister who had come to Alabama from Boston to help with voter registration, was beaten to death by a gang. President Johnson spoke to a joint session of Congress two days later, calling for a strong voting rights bill that would strengthen the Civil Rights Acts of 1957, 1960, and 1964. The president said,

> Our mission is at once the oldest and the most basic of this country: to right a wrong, to do justice, to serve man...The last time a President sent a civil rights bill to the Congress it contained a provision to protect voting rights in Federal elections. That civil rights bill was passed after eight long months of debate. And when that bill came to my desk from the Congress, the heart of the voting provision had been eliminated. This time, on this issue, there must be no delay, no hesitation and no compromise with our purpose.

Meanwhile, back in Alabama, Judge Frank Johnson overruled Governor Wallace, permitting the Selma march to take place on March 17. Americans from all over the country converged on Alabama—rabbis, priests, nuns, nurses, lawyers, maids, miners, whites, blacks, the young, and the old. They came in limousines,

On March 22, 1965, Dr. Martin Luther King, Jr., begins the second lap of the march to the state capitol at Montgomery. Several thousand troops were on hand to guard the marchers.

on battered buses, in wheelchairs, and on crutches, and some hitchhiked. All who came to Alabama came with one purpose in mind—to secure and to protect the rights of American voters no matter what their race, color, religion, sex, or national origin. As one elderly woman said, "Americans are not all bigots and racists."

President Johnson gave his support by sending federal troops. With twenty-two hundred troops protecting the marchers along the eighty-mile stretch, the walk began on the first day of spring 1965. Over twenty-five thousand people would participate in that massive protest, which is another landmark in civil rights history.

But the troop protection was not enough to save the life of a young housewife from Detroit named Mrs. Viola Liuzzo. She was murdered while driving demonstrators to the site.

Dr. Howard Thurman delivered this memorial tribute to her on March 30, 1965:

> The men who murdered Mrs. Liuzzo did not know her. They knew only one thing—she was a white woman from outside their region, but a white woman even as their mothers and sisters were white women and that her presence in their midst on such a mission as hers was a bitter judgment upon them and the angry world of hate and fear in which they were born and nurtured...

> She died.
> But we who live must do a harder thing
> Than dying is. For we must think!
> And ghosts shall drive us on.

Something good did come out of the seemingly endless suffering.
On August 6, 1965, President Johnson signed into law the Voting
Rights Act.

WATTS

Urban black youths were growing impatient. They were not
willing to wait for changes to happen. They were angry, and angry
people are not very reasonable.

Marquette Frye was arrested for driving under the influence of
alcohol. He was not particularly hostile, and the officer was reported
not to have been brutal in his arrest. No one is sure what happened,
but there was a fight between the white policeman and the black
youth. A crowd gathered, which soon turned into a raging mob,
and Watts, a ghetto area in Los Angeles, California, exploded.
Pent-up anger and frustration were released during days of looting
and burning.

*At the end of the five days of rioting in Watts, only firemen, police,
and National Guardsmen moved about.*

It took twenty-seven thousand local officers and guardsmen to bring the riots to an end. Thirty-four people were killed, and property damage totalled more than $40 million. Throughout the entire South, the nonviolent civil rights movement of 1957–1965 had not lost that many lives or property. In one day, Watts canceled out the miracle of the nonviolent movement and much of the goodwill that was growing between the races. Watts played into the hands of racists who stereotyped blacks as mindless, destructive brutes.

OPERATION BREADBASKET

Martin Luther King, Jr., had been aware that problems in the urban centers were strained to the breaking point. He had visited the northern ghettos in an effort to help ease tensions. King and his family had rented an apartment in one of the high-rise housing projects in Chicago. Within a month Dr. King sent his children back to Atlanta. He said the strain of living in those deplorable conditions was too much to ask of his family. What about the children and families who had to stay there?

In Chicago, the SCLC established "Operation Breadbasket," which was administered by a young disciple named Jesse Jackson. King had tried to encourage urban blacks to use peaceful protests to bring about changes, protests such as rent strikes, economic boycotts, demonstrations, and the use of the ballot. Although northern blacks could vote, they were apathetic and disinterested voters.

King's efforts were too late and not enough to stop the violence that erupted in Los Angeles and that spread over the country, and it saddened him tremendously.

Paratroopers rush to help an injured man in Vietnam.

VIETNAM

President Johnson was fighting two wars: his self-declared War on Poverty and the undeclared war in Vietnam. People began wondering how America had gotten involved in Vietnam.

United States involvement in the small Southeast Asian country began in 1954, when the French were driven out of Indochina by Communist-backed nationalists. Three new countries were formed at that time: Laos, Cambodia, and Vietnam. Vietnam was divided into two sections: the north was governed by the Communists, and the south was governed by a shaky democratic government. Around 1959, pro-Communist forces within South Vietnam escalated their guerrilla attacks on the country. Russia, China, and North Vietnam aided the guerrillas, who called themselves the Viet Cong.

President Eisenhower had pledged U.S. support to the fledgling democracy of South Vietnam, so military aid was sent. At first, American military advisers were sent to train South Vietnamese soldiers.

President Kennedy renewed the pledge in 1961 and sent more advisers. The guerrilla war continued as did American support. After the Gulf of Tonkin resolution, President Johnson escalated the war by increasing American bombing of North Vietnam, as well as by troop support. During his administration, more than 500,000 American soldiers were sent to Vietnam.

Protest marches began as soon as the United States sent the first advisers during the Kennedy administration. At first the protests were small. Then, as President Johnson committed more soldiers, the opposition to the war increased. By 1968, college campuses had exploded into violent protests against American involvement. There were flag burnings, draft-card burnings, and draft evasion. Many young men who were drafted refused to serve and went to live in Canada.

There were nearly 60,000 black soldiers in Vietnam in 1968. Ten percent of the U.S. forces in Vietnam were minorities. An overwhelming 20 percent of the troops were in combat units. Some believed that those statistics showed an unfair representation.

One of the early opponents to the Vietnam War was Martin Luther King, Jr. President Johnson responded angrily, accusing King of interfering in matters that did not concern him. Johnson privately told black leaders that he felt betrayed. The president believed that, since he had worked hard for civil rights, black leaders—especially King—owed him their loyalty. Many black leaders agreed, privately and publicly asking Dr. King to stop speaking out against the war. He was advised that if he could not say anything to support the president, then he should say nothing at all. King disagreed, saying, "We were taking the black young men who had been crippled by our society and sending them 8,000 miles away to guarantee liberties in Southeast Asia which they had not found in Southeast Georgia or East Harlem. So we have been repeatedly faced with the cruel irony of watching Negro and white boys on TV screens as they kill and die together for a nation that has been unable to seat them together in the same schools."

Stokely Carmichael, head of SNCC, standing on the hood of an automobile on the campus of Florida A & M University, speaks about black power and the Vietnam War.

Although he was criticized for it, Dr. King made the war his business, speaking out against it wherever he went. And even though he was under a great deal of critical pressure and FBI harassment, he never gave up on America, but other black leaders did. One was Stokely Carmichael.

STOKELY CARMICHAEL

The war, combined with continued resistance to civil rights in the South and unrest in the ghettos of the North, led to a drastic shift in black leadership. Blacks were becoming disillusioned by the nonviolent doctrines of King and were leaning more toward hard-line rhetoric.

Howard Zinn, the author of *SNCC*, describes Stokely Carmichael as "tall, slim, brown-skinned . . . gives the impression he would stride cool and smiling through Hell, philosophizing all the way." In 1965, twenty-five-year-old Carmichael was a SNCC field secretary in Lowndes County, Alabama. He was a veteran of the nonviolent protest and had taken his knocks and bumps during the freedom rides and Freedom Summer.

Carmichael was born in Trinidad, in the West Indies, and grew up in Harlem and the Bronx in New York City. He was graduated from Howard University in Washington, D.C., with a degree in philosophy but had joined SNCC in 1961 when he was a freshman. After graduation Carmichael continued to work with SNCC.

In Alabama, Carmichael formed Lowndes County Freedom Organization, a political party. His plan was to run a black candidate for the office of sheriff, therefore giving blacks a reason to register and vote. Alabama law required that a political party had to have a logo. Carmichael chose the black panther as a symbol of pride and power. The Blank Panther party candidate lost the election because of fear and terror tactics used by the opponents. But Carmichael scored it a victory because 3,900 new voters were registered.

Then in June 1965, James Meredith chose to march from the border of Tennessee to Jackson, Mississippi, to prove a point. On the first day out, the point was made. Meredith was shot and had to be taken to a Memphis hospital. All the major civil rights leaders met at the bedside of James Meredith: Stokely Carmichael, who had recently been elected director of SNCC; Floyd McKissick, director of CORE; Martin Luther King, Jr., of SCLC; Roy Wilkins of the NAACP; and Whitney Young, Jr., of the National Urban League.

Carmichael was militant in his stance and was backed by McKissick. Young and Wilkins were troubled by the new militant rhetoric, so the group agreed to disagree. Carmichael, McKissick, and King decided to go on with the march. Young and Wilkins returned to New York and refused to participate in the continuation of Meredith's March.

Stokely Carmichael knew how to use the language masterfully. When he needed it, he could use perfect grammar and diction. At other times, he chose to bark his demands in the harsh, shrill language of the streets. Either way, he was effective.

Whitney Young (top) and Roy Wilkins (below)

Some who attended a four-day conference on black power in 1967 are, seated from left: comedian Dick Gregory; Ron Karenga, leader of Black Nationalist Cultural Organization of the U.S.; H. Rap Brown, national chairman of SNCC; and Ralph Featherstone of SNCC.

Black Power!

Just as expected, the Meredith March was greeted with more "official brutality." The marchers were beaten, teargassed, and arrested. Among those beaten and arrested was Stokely Carmichael. When he was released, he said, "Never again will I take a beating without hitting back!" That night Carmichael addressed the group of tattered and bedraggled marchers. No longer was he a disciple of King and Gandhi. His philosophy and his style had changed. "We been saying freedom for six years," he said "and we ain't got nothin'. What we gonna start saying now is black power." An attempt was made to sing "We Shall Overcome," but it was drowned out by the chant of "Black Power!" "Black Power!" "Black Power!"

Immediately following the march, King took out a full-page advertisement in the *New York Times*, denouncing "black power." Carmichael published his definition of black power in the *New York Review of Books* on September 22, 1966:

> Politically, black power means what it has always meant to SNCC: the coming-together of black people to elect representatives and *to force those representatives to speak to their needs*. It does not mean merely putting black faces into office. A man or woman who is black and from the slums cannot be automatically expected to speak to the needs of black people. Most of the black politicians we see around the country today are not what SNCC means by black power. The power must be that of a community, and emanate from there.

The black power slogan was immediately adopted by CORE, and, along with the clenched fist, it became the symbol of the young militants who were no longer convinced that nonviolence could achieve their civil rights goals. They were giving notice that they were not willing to take any more beatings and to sing "We shall overcome . . . someday." They took to the streets and began shouting, "We want our rights, NOW. Power to the People!"

The Black Panthers

The black power movement produced several new leaders. On the West Coast, Bobby Seale and Huey Newton founded the Black Panther party of Oakland, California. They set up clinics and free breakfast programs in the ghetto and informed poor people about their legal rights. The Panthers made the same demands that civil rights leaders had been making for years: better housing, fair employment, equal opportunity, and a fair share of the American "apple pie." Whatever good they were trying to do in the ghetto was overshadowed by the image they projected. Their stern and bearded

H. Rap Brown was arrested in Virginia and held for extradition to Maryland, where he faced charges of inciting to riot and arson.

faces, huge Afro hairstyles, tough language, and militaristic style conjured up the specter of a black army. White people envisioned hordes of blacks rising up to "take over America" under their green, black, and red banner. Even what the "new militants" wore tended to alienate people—black shirts, black leather gloves, dark glasses, and black berets.

The Panthers were readily accepted by impressionable ghetto youths and by many disillusioned adults. They joined the organization by the hundreds, practiced martial arts, and asserted their manhood through their newfound black pride. Frustrations that had been suppressed for generations were bubbling close to the surface.

The Long, Hot Summer

A lot of things happened in 1967, but the ghetto riots are most remembered. As temperatures soared into the nineties, frustrations also reached the boiling point. All that was needed for the top to blow was a shove, a push, and an ill-timed arrest.

Racial rioting was not new in America. There had been riots since colonial times, but those in the late 1960s were unique. The violence was done by blacks and was contained within their neighborhoods. The people who were killed were almost exclusively blacks.

Stokely Carmichael called for black people to "off the honkeys." "The white man won't get off our backs, so we're going to knock him off."

Carmichael was followed as head of SNCC by twenty-three-year-old H. Rap Brown from Louisiana. He made Carmichael look mild. In Cambridge, Maryland, Brown gave a forty-minute speech on July 25. He thundered on about what had been happening around the country. What had happened in Detroit? It exploded. What had happened in New York? It exploded. What had happened in Harlem and Cincinnati? They exploded.

Brown cried: "If America don't come around we [are] going [to] burn it down, brother. . . . We are going to burn it down if we don't get our share of it."

In the summer of 1967, riots broke out in Detroit. Police with rifles are on the lookout for snipers who harassed the firefighters.

That night, Cambridge exploded! When the rioting was over, poor people were still poor, hungry people were still hungry, and unemployed people were still unemployed. When this was called to the attention of a young rioter, he unremorsefully replied that all those things were true, but he added that he felt satisfied.

President Johnson appointed the Kerner Commission to study the cause of the riots. Only a few people were surprised when the report showed that fair employment practices, decent housing, and more educational opportunities were what black people wanted and needed. How many times—how many ways—did black people have to keep saying the same things?

The riots, the growing militant movement, and student unrest on college campuses turned middle-class white Americans completely off. Their support and contributions stopped. The SCLC was in financial trouble, SNCC went bankrupt, and Dr. King's dream was turning into a nightmare.

THE DEATHS OF MARTIN AND BOBBY

Martin Luther King, Jr. was tired. He had been fighting for so long and was seriously questioning whether he should quit. Had it all been worth it, he wondered. Close friends assured him that he had made a difference. King, still believing in America and in integration, shifted his emphasis to the millions of poor in America of all colors. "Hunger knows no color," he said.

Uniting all the poor under a common cause was a monumental task, but such a coalition would have far-reaching political implications. King announced that, during the summer of 1968, there would be a mass poor-people's rally in Washington, D.C. He also continued to speak out against the war in Vietnam.

President Johnson had announced that he would not seek reelection, so the race was wide open. Robert Kennedy joined the antiwar movement and entered the presidential primaries. Blacks and Mexican Americans overwhelmingly supported Robert F. Kennedy's candidacy.

During the winter of 1968, Dr. King preached where his grandfather, father, and brother had served as pastors—Ebenezer Baptist Church in Atlanta. The theme of his sermon was based on summing up his life's work. He said that when his life was over, "I'd like for somebody to say that day that Martin Luther King, Jr., tried to love somebody."

Shortly afterward, King was asked to help the striking sanitation workers in Memphis, Tennessee, by coming there to lead a march. He agreed. What was to be a nonviolent protest march turned into a riot. King left Memphis feeling disgraced and defeated.

A few weeks later, King returned to Memphis and was determined to conduct a peaceful protest. He spoke to a large rally the night before the scheduled march. It was his last public address. "I've been to the mountaintop," he said "and I've seen the promised land! ... I may not get there with you, but I want you to know tonight that we as a people will get to the promised land! ... I'm not fearing any man! Mine eyes have seen the glory ... of the coming of the Lord!"

Martin Luther King, Jr., talking to the press just before his assassination.

Moments after Martin Luther King, Jr., was shot by an assassin's bullet, his aides point out from where the shot had come.

The next day, April 4, 1968, Martin Luther King, Jr., was killed by James Earl Ray, an escaped convict. The man who had always spoken to people of good reason was memorialized in burning cities. There were 168 riots throughout the country. The outcome was a shameful tribute to a man who had dedicated his life to peace and to racial harmony. Washington, D.C., was hardest hit by the arson and looting. More than 711 fires were set there, and ten people were killed. One white man was dragged from his car, then beaten and stabbed by an angry mob of black youths. Nationwide, twenty-six acts of arson were committed within the black community. Nearly 3,000 arrests and 21,270 injuries occurred, with more than 98 percent of them involving blacks. It took 55,000 soldiers to restore order.

Meanwhile, Martin Luther King, Jr.'s body was taken to Atlanta for burial. His funeral was attended by Eugene McCarthy, Nelson Rockefeller, Hubert Humphrey, Robert Kennedy, and many other political figures of the day. Georgia's governor, Lester Maddox, was conspicuously absent from the services. Maddox had refused to close Georgia's schools and had protested the lowering of the flag to half mast. (President Johnson had ordered that the flag go to half mast on all federal buildings in honor of Dr. King.) But Dr. King was beyond racism. Carved on King's tombstone are the words

Free at last, free at last;
Thank God, Almighty, I'm free at last.

There were those who clung faithfully to Dr. King's dream. They vowed never to let his vision of world peace and brotherhood be totally crushed. Coretta Scott King, the widow of Martin Luther King, Jr., became a principal leader in the nonviolent peace movement, and Ralph Abernathy, King's friend and co-worker, became president of the SCLC.

Reverend Martin Luther King, Jr.'s casket is pulled on a mule cart through the streets of Atlanta to funeral services at Morehouse College.

Senator Robert F. Kennedy was shot at the Ambassador Hotel in Los Angeles.

Two months later, on June 6, 1968, Robert Kennedy was fatally wounded by Sirhan B. Sirhan in Los Angeles. Kennedy had just won the California presidential primary and had addressed his enthusiastic campaign workers. When news spread that Kennedy was dead, the nation was too numb to react. How much more could the country endure?

Martin Luther King, Jr., was dead as was Robert Kennedy. The unpopular war in Vietnam was splitting the country in half. Americans had had their fill of violence. The mood of the nation was changing. Some contemporary political watchers marked 1968 as the end of the modern civil rights movement. Surely, the election of a conservative Republican did show that the country was ready for a different kind of leadership.

THE 1968 PRESIDENTIAL ELECTION

In July 1968, Richard M. Nixon was nominated as the Republican presidential candidate in Atlanta. His nomination was not surprising,

Richard M. Nixon won the Republican presidential nomination in 1968.

and nothing out of the ordinary happened. The convention was described by reporters as "predictable" and "downright boring."

The Democratic convention was held several weeks later in Chicago at the International Amphitheater, and it was anything but boring. Antiwar demonstrators had begun rallying outside the Democratic headquarters days in advance. Mayor Richard Daley was not taking any chances. He had the manholes around the amphitheater sealed with tar and a seven-foot barbed wire fence put up around the hall. More than 11,000 policemen were put on twelve-hour shifts, and 5,500 National Guardsmen were alerted.

The protesters—mostly white, middle-class youths between the ages of eighteen and twenty-five—gathered in Lincoln Park on Chicago's North Side. After playing guitars and singing peace songs, they gave speeches and read poetry. At 11:00 P.M., police officers asked the group to obey the curfew. Only a few protestors refused and were arrested. The next day, which was Sunday, August 6, 1968, 2,000 Yippies (the Youth International party) and an assortment

Police attempt to disperse demonstrators outside the Democratic convention headquarters in Chicago.

of other protest groups gathered in the park. Jerry Rubin, leader of the Yippies, had planned to nominate a 125-pound hog named Pigusus for president. Rubin was arrested. The crowd began to chant, "Hell no, we won't go" and "Oink! Oink!"

At curfew time, police officers charged the group and swung nightsticks to evict forcibly the demonstrators. The same thing happened on Monday night. On Tuesday night, seventy priests and ministers erected a large cross, and the crowd, which had grown to over eighty thousand, sang "We Shall Overcome." Meanwhile, 300 policemen charged the protesters with tear gas. Many of the protesters responded by throwing stones and calling the police "pigs." Inside the amphitheater, the Democratic convention was under way. But the news media seemed more interested in what was going on outside than in what was going on inside.

The climax came on Thursday, August 10, 1968. A peaceful anti-Vietnam march had been planned by David Dellinger of the Committee to End the War. The march was to move from the Grant Park bandstand to the amphitheater. But Chicago's mayor, Richard Daley, said that there would be no march, peaceful or otherwise, and there was none. What happened has been called a "police riot."

The antiwar demonstrators were confronted by the police at Michigan Avenue and Balbo Drive across from the Conrad Hilton Hotel, which was the headquarters of the three Democratic presidential candidates. The crowd taunted the police, yelling, "Oink! Oink!" and "Seig Heil!" Suddenly, something snapped. The police attacked the protesters with swift efficiency, swinging their nightsticks forcefully. Men and women were dragged by their hair, feet, or arms and thrown into waiting wagons. It did not matter that some of the demonstrators were news personnel, convention workers, or innocent bystanders. Anyone in the way was clubbed, beaten, and taken to jail. The scene lasted for eighteen minutes, but one reporter called it "eighteen minutes of hell."

All this was going on while Hubert Humphrey was being nominated as the Democratic presidential candidate. For a long time, Humphrey had been the advocate of peace and civil rights and champion of the average person. After the Chicago fiasco, the average American turned to Nixon. And those who did not like either Nixon's or Humphrey's position had a third choice—George Wallace.

George Wallace, the former governor of Alabama, ran as president on the American Independent party ticket. He said that he represented people who were dissatisfied with both parties. Nixon was elected as the thirty-seventh president of the United States in November 1968. Wallace, however, picked up 9.9 million votes, and not all (13.5 percent) of his votes were from Southerners.

Also noted in the 1968 election was Ronald Reagan, a former actor and Democrat-turned-Republican, who was elected governor of California on the basis of his ultraconservative ideas. It was a clear indication that the country was shifting its political views. The shift would take another decade, but 1968 marked the beginning of what has been called "the white backlash."

MOVING ON UP A LITTLE HIGHER

In his 1969 inaugural address, President Nixon described the state of the nation: "We find ourselves rich in goods, but ragged in spirit; reaching with magnificent precision for the moon, but falling into raucous discord on earth. We are caught in war, wanting peace. We are torn by divisions, wanting unity."

Exactly six months later, on July 20, 1969, Neil Armstrong walked on the moon. As he stepped onto the moon's surface, he said, "That's one step for man; one giant leap for mankind." Back on earth, schools and neighborhoods remained segregated. Blacks and other minorities had not reached the level of equality that would make them first-class citizens.

Yet, undeniably, changes were taking place; some were small, while others were dramatized by the press. Black mayors were being elected in major cities, such as Carl Stokes in Cleveland, Ohio, and Richard Hatcher in Gary, Indiana. Even in the Deep South, Charles Evers was elected mayor of Fayette, Mississippi, where his brother, Medgar Evers, had been killed a few years earlier.

Shirley Chisholm of New York was the first black woman to be elected to the House of Representatives; Edward Brooke of Massachusetts would hold the honor of being the first black senator since Reconstruction; and Thurgood Marshall was appointed to the Supreme Court in 1967.

Charles Evers served as mayor of Fayette, Mississippi, and Shirley Chisholm of New York was the first black woman to be elected to the House of Representatives.

As blacks advanced and gained their civil rights, so did other minorities, including women. They advanced in education, housing, business, industry, and banking. In the words of the old spiritual song, they were "Moving On Up a Little Higher."

The Generation Gap

In the late 1960s and early 1970s, a number of white youths began a rebellion against the "Establishment." Young college students were choosing not to follow in the footsteps of their fathers and mothers and to do things the way they had always been done. Some of these youths—called hippies—displayed their rebellion by wearing wild clothing, growing beards and long hair, dropping out of society, living in communes, and using drugs. The split was called the Generation Gap. As the differences grew between the two age groups, so did the conflicts between fathers and sons and between mothers and daughters. And the gap was widened by the differences over the Vietnam War.

Just as all youths were not hippies, all antiwar demonstrators were not young. A diverse group of antiwar protesters got involved early and lost their jobs, sacrificed their careers, and often went to jail or paid high fines. The group expanded to include priests, rabbis, ministers, performers, businessmen, educators, and politicians.

Antiwar Extremism

Vietnam seemed to be the target for youthful opposition; racism, however, was also a rallying point around which young idealists could gather.

A few of the antiwar pacifists burned their draft cards and fled the country rather than serve in the military. A few young men chose to serve jail terms or to pay stiffly imposed fines. One of the most controversial antiwar demonstrators was Muhammad Ali, an Olympic gold medalist and heavyweight boxing champion of the world.

In 1967, Ali was drafted but refused to serve in Vietnam. As a member and minister of the Black Muslims, he refused military duty on the basis of his religion. He was found guilty, stripped of his heavyweight title, and given a jail sentence. Once the war ended, Ali came back to recapture the heavyweight title that many said had been unjustly taken from him.

As with any protest movement, there were extremists. It was an act of extremism when National Guardsmen overreacted to an antiwar protest and killed four young demonstrators at Kent State

Thousands of people rallied against the war in Vietnam in front of the United Nations building in New York City in 1966. In 1967, Muhammad Ali, then known as Cassius Clay, refused to be drafted into the armed forces. He is shown with his attorney. Later he was drafted, but refused to serve in Vietnam.

University. But it was an extremist of the peace movement who bombed the Army Mathematics Research Center at the University of Wisconsin, killing an innocent young scientist.

The Youth International party (Yippies)—represented by Jerry Rubin—and the Weathermen were organizations that leaned toward extremism within the peace movement.

The Twenty-sixth Amendment

An end to the war was inevitable. But something else resulted from the war protests. The war was being fought by eighteen- to twenty-year-olds who were too young to vote. On June 21, 1971, Nixon signed the Twenty-sixth Amendment, which gave the right to vote to eighteen-year-olds, a right they had earned with their blood. Based on the conduct of the youth at that time, opponents predicted that eighteen-year-olds would not be responsible voters.

Anti-war demonstrations spread throughout the United States to protest American involvement in Vietnam.

That was an erroneous assumption. American's youth today are among the most well-informed voters in the world.

After vigorous negotiations that were led by Secretary of State Henry Kissinger, a cease-fire agreement was signed in Paris on January 27, 1973. For America, the war in Vietnam was technically over. American troops unceremoniously returned home. It was an awful time for them, having neither won nor lost the war. Vietnam veterans finally would be given a welcome-home celebration in several major American cities, including Chicago, years later.

For the people of Vietnam, their troubles were just beginning. Fighting continued between the South Vietnamese and the Communists, who, in May 1975, took over the South Vietnamese government.

Motorcycle police stand by as students board buses in Boston.

BUSING

The crisis in the northern cities drove out middle-class whites, as well as the growing numbers of middle-class black families. Whites moved to the suburbs to look for a better life, leaving the cities to the poor and the underprivileged. This "white flight" cost the cities thousands of tax dollars, which affect inner-city education and businesses. In 1970, there were still "separate and unequal" school systems all over America. The inner-city schools were in poor condition because they had little or no money to keep them going.

In October 1969, fifteen years after the Brown decision, the Supreme Court ruled unanimously that school districts must end racial segregation at once and "with all deliberate speed." To achieve this goal, a busing plan was developed. In 1971, the Supreme Court approved the strategy of busing to achieve racial balance in schools. As with the Brown decision, there was a great deal of resistance to the ruling.

Mrs. Edna Wade, president of the Unified Concerned Citizens of Alabama, a group opposed to busing to achieve integration, holds up the twenty-dollar contribution she received from George Wallace, governor of Alabama.

In March 1972, President Nixon asked Congress to pass a moratorium on busing, but Congress declined. Nixon accused federal judges of "overreaching themselves and helping to generate turmoil in local communities." It was an election year, and he was appealing to the "silent majority." George Wallace was in the presidential race and was doing very well by speaking out against busing, but an attempted assassination paralyzed Wallace and ended his candidacy. Still, the conservative swing that had started in the late 1960s was still moving to the political Right.

Public dissatisfaction with busing often resulted in violent protests such as the one in Boston in 1974. Advocates of busing say that they were willing to admit that busing is not an ideal solution to the school desegregation problem. But until an alternative is found, busing is the only method that gives the Brown decision any substance.

Those who argue against busing point out that it is costly, that it destroys the neighborhood-school concept, and that it creates more hostility than it resolves. The argument continues with the idea that schools can be "separate and equal" today because segregation is not mandatory.

Busing is a double-edged sword. Busing is costly, but it helps to bring children together who otherwise would never have the experience of knowing each other. Busing brings children together under strained conditions that increase white flight and white backlash. Whatever the opinion, the fact remains that, where there is busing, there is school integration. Where there is no busing, schools remain separate and unequal.

An anti-busing rally in Boston.

The only true solution is, obviously, integrated neighborhoods. During the 1980s, tens of thousands of blacks, Hispanics, Asians, and other minorities moved to the suburbs surrounding major U.S. cities. This helped cause a sharp reduction in segregation in those metropolitan areas. Unfortunately, the reduction was all in the suburban areas, with the cities themselves remaining heavily segregated. It is still too soon to tell whether the suburbs will evolve into truly integrated neighborhoods, or whether they will simply expand into suburban minority ghettoes. If the latter is the case, forced integration of the schools via busing will remain the only option.

Police cars were sometimes necessary to escort school buses used for school integration.

Women took their cause into the streets as they demonstrated for equal treatment under the law.

THE WOMEN'S MOVEMENT

Black people's struggle for civil rights encouraged other minority groups also to seek their rights. Legislation was passed between 1930 and 1970 that helped to elevate the status not only of blacks but also of Hispanics, Asians, Jews, and women. But are women a minority?

One definition of "minority" is people who are socially excluded, economically oppressed, and politically powerless. Using that definition, women make up the largest minority in America. When the modern feminist movement was revitalized in the mid-1960s, there were very few female corporate executives, military officers, engineers, and brain surgeons. It was difficult for a woman to buy anything on credit without her husband's consent. Women were expected to marry before the age of twenty-five or to live their lives as "old maids." Women had very few choices.

Working women were subject to these three stereotypes:

1. Some women have to work because of divorce or death; working women who are married reflect negatively on their husbands, who cannot take care of their families.

2. Unmarried working women are looking for a husband—usually, the boss.

3. Married women who are helping their husbands through professional school or who are helping them start a business are acceptable because it is not a permanent situation. As soon as the husband gets his professional degree or gets his business off the ground, the wife stops working.

Those women who worked because they wanted to build a career were frowned on by society.

How did such ideas form? It was a matter of conditioning, beginning in early childhood. The parameters of womanhood and manhood were set by the games that children played. Little girls played house, teacher, or nurse. Little boys played with science kits, trucks, and doctor kits. Girls and boys were expected to behave in certain ways. By the time that children reached adolescence, the male and female roles were well defined.

Betty Friedan's *The Feminine Mystique*

There has always been a small group of rebellious women who refuse to accept society's limitations. From these scattered rebels came the first rumblings of malcontent. In 1963, Betty Friedan wrote *The Feminine*

Mystique. Friedan encouraged women to challenge the traditional roles that society had set for them, and this they did! The book was a best-seller. Some credit Friedan with being the person who launched the modern feminist movement. One of the primary targets that women chose to challenge was unfair employment practices.

What follows is a typical 1940 scenario. Two colleges graduates, one woman and one man, were hired by a school district to teach seventh grade. Both teachers had the same education ad experience. Twenty years later, both educators went back to school to get degrees in administration, but it was the man who was promoted to assistant superintendent. The overqualified woman was still teaching seventh grade and earning less than her colleague.

Another common problem that women experienced was unequal pay for equal work. In 1962, two people sat side by side in an accounting firm doing the same work. Both employees worked the same number of hours. However, the man earned more money than did the woman.

Some of the more important women's issues were clouded by bra burnings and other displays of female hostility. Robin Morgan, a

Betty Friedan founded NOW, the National Organization for Women, in 1966.

television actress, crashed the 1968 Miss America Pageant by dragging a trail of burning bras on stage. Morgan was also the founder of the Women's International Terrorist Conspiracy from Hell (WITCH).

Early feminist protests and demonstrations were dismissed as silly, but they helped to jar men and women out of their complacency. Although the early women's organizations were too radical for the average woman, and although the issues were misinterpreted and misunderstood by most, a growing number of women were beginning to see a need for change. As the women's movement gained in popularity, efforts were made to discredit it by portraying "Women's Libbers" as bitter, angry, anti-male, and anti-family WITCHES.

Through the efforts of persistent feminist groups, women continued to organize and to select highly qualified representatives to speak for their cause. Soon the women's movement was taken seriously. Elected officials gave women's rights the attention it deserved. Going into the 1970s, women had one collective demand: equality NOW.

Suffragettes line up on a New York street before a rally in 1915.

Bella Abzug   Shirley Chisholm

The National Organization for Women (NOW)

The National Organization for Women (NOW)—founded in 1966 by Betty Friedan and a group of other feminists—emerged in the 1970s as the strongest group representing the feminist movement in America. As a politically oriented organization, NOW's aim was "to establish full equality for women in all areas of life." Equality meant the right to expect the same pay as a man for doing the same quality and amount of work, as well as equality in education and business opportunities.

Of course, NOW was not acceptable to all women. Some felt that the organization was too militant; others felt that it was not militant enough. Those who believed that NOW was too radical used the same nineteenth-century arguments that were used to oppose women's suffrage. Those who felt that NOW was not militant enough argued that women had been denied their rights for too long and that it was time to take what was rightfully theirs.

Bella Abzug and Shirley Chisholm, two congresswomen from New York, were among the first congressional leaders who outspokenly advocated women's rights. Chisholm, a black woman, also ran a serious campaign for president in 1972.

The Equal Rights Amendment (ERA)

In 1970, the Equal Rights Amendment (ERA) was passed by the U.S. House of Representatives and the Senate. The amendment stated: "Equality of rights under the law shall not be denied or abridged by the United States or any state on account of sex."

The amendment needed to be ratified by thirty-eight states before it could become a part of the Constitution. Supporters of the ERA had until 1979 to achieve that goal. By mid-1976, thirty-four states had approved the ERA, with Indiana ratifying it in 1977. These states included:

Alaska	Maryland	Oregon
California	Massachusetts	Pennsylvania
Colorado	Michigan	Rhode Island
Connecticut	Minnesota	South Dakota
Delaware	Montana	Tennessee
Hawaii	Nebraska	Texas
Idaho	New Hampshire	Vermont
Indiana	New Jersey	Washington
Iowa	New Mexico	West Virginia
Kansas	New York	Wisconsin
Kentucky	North Dakota	Wyoming
Maine	Ohio	

The National Women's Conference

The National Women's Conference was held November 18 – 21, 1977. Women gathered in Houston, Texas, to work out an organized play of

First Lady Rosalynn Carter and two former first ladies, Betty Ford and Lady Bird Johnson, attended the opening session of the National Women's Conference in Houston.

action. Their "Declaration of American Women" stated,

> We are here to move history forward. We are women from every State and Territory in the Nation. We are women of different ages, beliefs, and life-styles. We are women of many economic, social, political, racial, ethnic, cultural, educational, and religious backgrounds.
>
> We are married, single, widowed, and divorced. We are mothers and daughters. We are sisters.
>
> We can vote and own property. We work in the home, in our communities, and in every occupation. We are 40 percent of the labor force. We are in the arts, sciences, professions, and politics. We raise children, govern States, head businesses and institutions, climb mountains, explore the ocean depths, and reach toward the moon.
>
> Our lifespan has increased to more than 75 years. We have become a majority of the population, 51.3 percent, and by the 21st Century, we shall be an even larger majority.
>
> But despite some gains made in the past 200 years, our dream of equality is still withheld from us and millions of women still face a daily reality of discrimination, limited opportunities, and economic hardship.

During those four days in November, women developed their National Plan of Action, which included their concerns on the following issues: rape, minority women, media representation, insurance, homemakers, international affairs, health, education, elected offices, disabled women, finance, child care, business, arts and humanities, credit, and passage of the ERA.

The group was addressed by First Lady Rosalynn Carter, former first ladies Lady Bird Johnson and Betty Ford, and Coretta Scott King, the widow of Dr. Martin Luther King, Jr. Susan B. Anthony, the grandniece of Susan B. Anthony (the nineteenth-century suffragist), also spoke to the group. Enthusiasm for the ERA ran high. As one supporter said, "If I should die, don't send me flowers. Just send me three more States."

On the final day of the conference, three hundred delegates left the convention floor in protest against the ERA and other women's issues that the conference had voted to support. The group was led by Joan Gubbins, a state senator from Indiana.

"Failure [of ERA] is impossible," responded a speaker at the podium. There was thunderous applause.

The Failure of the Equal Rights Amendment

In the fall of 1977, failure of the ERA did seem impossible. But it did fail. Gloria Steinem, editor of *MS* magazine, was a major spokesperson for the ERA. Opposition to the ERA was led by Phyllis Schlafly, a lawyer from Alton, Illinois, and founder of the Stop-ERA movement.

Only three more states were needed to ratify the ERA to make it a law. But statistics showed that support for the amendment had dropped from 65 percent in 1976 to 56 percent in 1977. Supporters were shocked when the amendment failed in Missouri, Nevada, North Carolina, Virginia, and Florida. In Arkansas, Georgia, and Mississippi the amendment was either deadlocked in committee or destined to fail. It was obvious that the amendment would not pass by the 1979 deadline.

Congresswomen Elizabeth Holtzman, a Democrat from New York, helped push legislation through that extended the deadline for ratification to June 30, 1982.

Phyllis Schlafly proved to be a formidable opponent. The mood of the country had shifted dramatically from liberal to conservative. The election of Ronald Reagan to the presidency made the critical difference. President Reagan and First Lady Nancy Reagan opposed the ERA. The Stop-ERA movement gained momentum and blocked its ratification in critical states. These are the states that did not pass the ERA:

Alabama	Illinois	North Carolina
Arizona	Louisiana	Oklahoma
Arkansas	Mississippi	South Carolina
Florida	Missouri	Utah
Georgia	Nevada	Virginia

ERA supporters march to the Illinois state capital to rally for passage of the ERA amendment.

Phyllis Schlafly, national leader of the "Stop the Equal Rights Amendment" movement, was successful in helping to defeat passage of the amendment in Illinois.

Defeat of the ERA was a major setback for the modern feminist movement. The defeat also marked a shift in strategy for those still determined to win true equality for women. Like civil rights activists around the country, women moved off the streets and into legislative bodies and board rooms to fight their battles. With the increased conservatism of successive Republican administrations, grass-roots organization has taken the place of federal support and funding.

Among the major concerns of women's rights activists of the 1990s are employment opportunities, economic conditions, health care, and legal rights. Although progress is being made, the future is not all rosy. For example:

Although it is no longer legal to discriminate between men and women when advertising for and filling job vacancies, a woman still earns just 70 cents to a man's $1 in stereotypically female jobs. Employers still resist giving reasonable maternity leave with pay and job protection, and in-house employee day-care facilities are almost nonexistent. And while women have increased their participation by 300 percent to 400 percent in such fields as medicine, law, and management since the early 1970s, fewer than one-half of 1 percent of the most senior corporate officers are women. Women suffer after they leave the work force, too: They are only half as likely as men to work in jobs offering pensions, and working women are seriously penalized by Social Security, the federal retirement system.

Women's activists are also mobilizing to increase awareness of women's health issues. In many clinical tests for any number of health problems, medical researchers routinely use only male subjects. Because male and female physiology differs greatly, this means that the benefits for women remain unknown. A focus for the future will be to reduce this bias against women in health research. One promising sign came in 1991, when the National Institute of Health announced a ten-year comprehensive study on women's health-care issues. This study, which will involve hundreds of thousands of women, is designed to study all major causes of illness and death among women.

Fortunately or unfortunately, many women's health rights center on their reproduction rights. The Supreme Court ruling of *Roe v. Wade* in 1972 guaranteed women the right to an abortion in the case of unwanted pregnancy. Many women hailed this as a major victory; just as many others saw it as a grievous loss that amounted to little less than sanctioned murder. The Pro-Life/Pro-Choice debate has not cooled in twenty years, and the Supreme Court's *Webster* decision of July 1989 (which opened the way for states to pass laws restricting abortion) only helped fan the flames of discord. On this one issue at least, women themselves are sharply divided—and show very little sign of reaching a friendly agreement.

Representatives from the National Organization of Women march in front of the White House to carry their message to the president.

Other Supreme Court rulings have seemingly pitted the rights of women against those of their unborn children. The Civil Rights Act of 1964 and the Pregnancy Discrimination Act of 1978 supposedly guaranteed that women could not be excluded from any jobs they were able to do because of their gender, pregnancy, or possible pregnancy. Yet some employees routinely restricted women of child-bearing age from jobs whose environmental hazards might harm their fetuses, should the women become pregnant. The Supreme Court's decision in the case of *UAW v. Johnson Controls, Inc.* in 1991 unequivocally ruled this practice illegal. In the words of Justice Harry Blackmun, "Decisions about the welfare of future children must be left to the parents who conceive, bear, support and raise them rather than to the employers who hire those parents." The question remains—is this a victory for women, or a defeat for children? And must women's rights and children's rights always be in conflict?

Many Hollywood celebrities joined women's rights activists in a pro-choice march on Washington, D.C., in 1989.

One especially troubling area of women's vs. children's rights concerns a pregnant woman's use of illegal drugs. Health and legal experts know that alcohol and drug abuse by a pregnant woman can cause devastating damage to the fetus. The question is, what should be done about it? Should pregnant women who engage is behavior that is known to be dangerous to their unborn children be prosecuted by the law? Should they be forced to undergo treatment? Where do the rights of the woman end, and the rights of the fetus begin? These are controversial and troubling questions—for which there are no easy answers.

Violence is yet another rallying cry for women's rights activists. Rape and physical abuse account for fully one-third of all emergency room admittances in some urban hospitals. Current legislation before Congress would make violence against women a civil rights violation and would significantly toughen federal penalties for such violence. Countering such promising legislation are actions such as those by the Arkansas Supreme Court, which in 1990 struck down every domestic-violence law on the book, making Arkansas the only state in the union in which a woman can't get a protective order against a violent spouse.

And so women's rights activists continue the struggle. Women are entering the political arena in ever increasing numbers, and are voting for candidates who support women's rights. The goals are the same as they were in Susan B. Anthony's day—freedom, equality, and justice. And as long as there is discrimination based on sex, there will always be a women's movement.

CHILDREN'S RIGHTS

The United Nations designated 1979 the Year of the Child to focus world attention on children. Twenty years earlier, the United Nations General Assembly had adopted the Declaration of the Rights of Children. It stated that the world's children had rights to enjoy special protection; to be given opportunities to develop in a healthy and normal manner and in conditions of freedom; to have a name and a nationality from birth; to enjoy adequate nutrition, housing, recreation and medical services; to receive education and care if handicapped; to grow up wherever possible in the care of parents; to receive education; to be protected against neglect and cruelty; to be protected from any form of discrimination; and to be brought up in a spirit of understanding, tolerance, friendship among peoples, peace and universal brotherhood.

Despite such stirring resolutions, children are far from enjoying the rights they deserve in our society. Judging from statistics alone,

Child labor laws of the early twentieth century put an end to practices such as this young boy's long days working in a cotton mill.

America's children may well be our country's most disadvantaged minority. At the beginning of the 1990s, the children's rights scorecard read as follows:

- 1 of 8 American children under age 12 does not get enough to eat on any given day;
- Nearly 1 of 4 American children under age 6 lives in poverty;
- Reports of child abuse have soared from 600,000 in 1979 to 2.4 million in 1989;
- Between 1978 and 1987, federal spending on programs for the elderly rose 52 percent, while spending on children dropped 4 percent;
- The United States is one of only four countries (the others are Iran, Iraq, and Bangladesh) that still execute juvenile criminal offenders;
- The nation's infant mortality rate of 9.1 deaths for 1,000 live births is worse than that of 17 other developed countries.

Statistics for minority children are even worse. Forty-three percent of all black children are born in poverty; in some Indian tribes, more than 80 percent of children live below official government poverty lines. And in some urban areas, the infant mortality rate for blacks and Hispanic babies is twice that of white babies.

The conclusions are obvious. Children who are poorly clothed, poorly housed, poorly fed, and poorly treated cannot develop into responsible, productive citizens. It would seem to be in any government's best interests to care first and foremost for its young. And yet, perhaps because children do not represent a politically or economically powerful voting bloc in the United States, their most basic rights are often shamefully ignored.

Attempts have been made to right the wrongs. In the 1970s, Congress launched its Special Supplemental Food Program for Women, Infants and Children (WIC). WIC was an acknowledgment that good nutrition is essential for healthy infant development—and that babies have no control over the financial abilities of their parents to provide them with wholesome foods. WIC offered mothers food vouchers, nutrition classes, and medical care—all for about $30 a month. But budget cuts during the Reagan and Bush administrations squeezed government funds so tight, that by 1990 less than 60 percent of eligible women and children were receiving WIC benefits.

Budget cuts have also been responsible for a decline in childhood health care. With the high costs of medical care, many parents cannot afford even the most basic check-ups and inoculations so vital to childhood health—and there is no consistent, across-the-board government health insurance plan to help out.

Head Start is one government program that has proven early intervention can help. Head Start is a quality preschool for disadvantaged children that also includes annual medical and dental screenings. Although President Bush has pledged enough funding to put every eligible child into a Head Start program, as of 1990 only about 20 percent of those children were being served.

In general, federal spending has lagged far behind need when it comes to children's and family rights over the past decade. In 1990, President Bush vetoed the Family and Medical Leave Act, which would have guaranteed workers up to twelve weeks a year of unpaid leave to care for newborns, adopted children, or sick family members. But children's rights advocates do exist in Congress. In 1990, Congress finally passed a compromise version of the Act for Better Child Care after a two-year debate. And despite the administration's continued opposition, family-leave legislation was back on the Congressional agenda in 1991.

The biggest gain for children's rights has taken place on an international level. In September 1990, the World Summit for Children was sponsored by the United Nations in New York City. This summit was widely hailed as among the most important gatherings ever

Poverty and racial discrimination hit the young of the United States particularly hard.

called by the nations of the world. Out of it came the international Convention on the Rights of the Child, a fifty-four-article document that adds children to the ranks of those whose human rights must be protected by their governments. Among the rights covered in the convention are the right to adequate housing, health services, child care, education, and recreational and cultural activities. National leaders from around the world endorsed a ten-year plan to reduce mortality rates, fight poverty, increase access to immunizations, and improve education.

The Convention of the Rights of the Child has been made international law by the fifty countries that have ratified it so far. As of 1991, the United States was not one of those countries.

RIGHTS OF THE DISABLED

It was not until World War II that disabled people, some of them veterans, began seeking rights that were guaranteed to them by the Constitution. Too many people were uninformed or misinformed about disabled persons, which led to widespread prejudice and stereotyping. Disabled persons were frequently victims of neglect and abuse and their rights were disregarded.

Beginning in the 1960s, disabled-rights advocates won several important legal cases. In the *Pennsylvania Association of Retarded Citizens v. Commonwealth of Pennsylvania* case, fourteen retarded children were denied free public education. In its decree, the court recognized the right of mentally retarded children to have access to public education. That was a landmark decision because, up until that time, mentally retarded children were sent to residential boarding schools or to state hospitals where they were often mistreated.

The *Wyatt v. Stickney* case involved the treatment of all mentally ill and mentally retarded persons who were confined in Alabama institutions. Handicapped persons were usually sent to nursing homes, to state hospitals, or were abandoned on the streets to beg for their needs. The judge ruled that public institutions that purported to provide care and treatment for the handicapped had to do so humanely.

Meanwhile, Congress passed legislation to support the court's rulings. The Education of All Handicapped Children Act committed federal financial assistance to the disableds' right to education. The act required each state to guarantee "free appropriate public education" and an "individualized education program" to all its disabled children from the ages of three to eighteen by September 1, 1978, and to all handicapped children from the ages of three to twenty-one by September 1, 1980. The act further stipulated that there "shall be no unnecessary removal of children with disabilities from the normal school environment."

The Rehabilitation Act of 1973 has been called the disableds' "Bill of Rights." The act prohibited discrimination against the handicapped "under any program or activity receiving federal assistance." This act changed the lives of millions of Americans. To mention a few examples, all public buildings are now required to have ramps for those who cannot climb stairs, parking lots have designated parking spots for the handicapped, and many elevators have floors marked in Braille.

The efforts of individuals such as these led to the successful passage of the Americans with Disabilities Act of 1990.

Accessibility to public transportation and public buildings is a leading concern for disabled rights activists.

The Developmentally Disabled Assistance and Bill of Rights Act of 1975 addressed the problem of finding alternatives to the almost automatic practice of institutionalizing the disabled. The act required that each state design a plan "to eliminate inappropriate placement in institutions of persons with developmental disabilities and to improve the quality of care and the state of surroundings of persons for whom institutional care is appropriate."

Disabled rights suffered setbacks in the 1980s, even though experts estimated that some 43 million Americans, or about one-sixth of the population, had some sort of disability. Several court cases reversed some of the earlier rulings. In addition, cutbacks in federally sponsored handicapped programs curtailed many services. Handicapped-rights advocates continued to work for programs designed to improve services for the disabled in the areas of housing, treatment, training, education, transportation, employment, counseling and recreation, but essentially handicapped people were protected by only a patchwork of state and local laws.

Then, in 1990, President Bush signed into law the Americans with Disabilities Act, which some advocates say is the most sweeping civil-rights statute since the 1964 Civil Rights Act. The Americans with Disabilities Act offers a nationwide agenda for providing America's disabled with new employment opportunities and greater access to public accommodations, public and private transportation, and telecommunications networks. The basic provisions for the act begin going into effect in 1992 and will:

- Prohibit firms with more than 25 employees (to be reduced to 15 in 1994) from discriminating in hiring, firing, training, promoting, and providing benefits for workers with most physical or mental impairments;

- Outlaw tests likely to screen out handicapped job applicants. Employees would still be allowed to determine a worker's ability to perform a specific job;

- Guarantee disabled people the chance to partake "fully and equally," in a business's services and goods. Among other things, this would require restaurants and stores to widen doorways and provide ramps for wheelchairs (or provide door buzzers to summon a salesperson's help in entering); and would require stores to have sales help on hand to read prices to visually impaired customers, for example.

- Require that inner city buses be made accessible to the handicapped.

While the nation's disabled and their advocates cheered the new Act, some feared a taxpayer backlash when the cost for implementing its provisions were totaled. To counter confusion and complaints, resource networks were set up as soon as the law was enacted to assist businesses and public agencies in meeting those provisions. Despite concerns about its implementation, the American with Disabilities Act should go a long way toward making all of us aware of the rights—and the abilities—of the disabled members of our society.

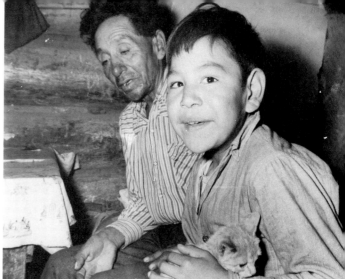

A member of the American Indian Movement (AIM) stands guard outside Sacred Heart Catholic Church in Wounded Knee, South Dakota (left). The life expectancy in some Indian tribes is just forty-five years.

AMERICAN INDIAN CIVIL RIGHTS

For many years, American Indians were the "forgotten people." Classroom textbooks hardly mentioned them after 1890, and neither fiction nor nonfiction represented the various Native American cultures accurately. Hollywood was responsible for creating many of the Indian myths; also, Indians did not write their own history until recently.

After being silent for half a century and being inspired by black American's advances in civil rights, Indians gathered in Chicago in 1961. Members from sixty-seven tribes met and issued their demands:

> We believe in the inherent right of all people to retain spiritual and cultural values, and that the free exercise of these values is necessary to the normal development of any people. . . The Indians ask for assistance, technical and financial, for the time needed, however long that may be, to regain in the America of the space age some measure of the adjustment they enjoyed as the original possessors of the native land.

As civil rights legislation was passed, it gave Indians many rights that they had been denied. Still, Indians had needs that were not being covered. For example, they held the Bureau of Indian Affairs in contempt. Indian leaders accused bureau officials of being insensitive, inefficient, and ineffective.

In 1973, militant members of the American Indian Movement (AIM) seized the village of Wounded Knee in South Dakota and demanded a Senate investigation of the Bureau. They also requested that the 371 treaties between the United States and the various Indian nations be reviewed. In response, President Nixon asked Congress to set up the Indian Trust Counsel Authority and also to provide credit and financial aid to Indians.

Indians found that their organizing helped. Dropping many of their tribal differences, they formed national organizations that monitored Indian interests: National Congress of American Indians; Arrow, Incorporated; the Indian Rights Association; and the Association of Indian Affairs.

Militant leaders of the Menominee tribe were not satisfied with the slow steps made by the government, so they seized a Catholic seminary in Wisconsin in January 1975. The religious order that owned the property agreed to turn it over to the Indians to be used as a medical facility.

In the spring of 1977, the Navaho Indians joined with other tribes in the New Mexico area to form the Council of Energy Resource Tribes. Their purpose was to protest eleven bills before Congress that were designed to utilize Indian lands protected by treaty. That same year, one thousand Indians participated in a three-thousand-mile trek called the "Longest Walk to Washington." Their leaders spoke with President Jimmy Carter regarding Indian concerns.

Education has always been key to Indian success in a predominantly white world. In 1976, the Indian Self-Determination Act was passed, an act that essentially encouraged Native Americans to take their education into their own hands. For the first time, the federal government seemed to be admitting that perhaps assimilation into white culture wasn't the only way and that traditional Indian lessons and languages had a place in the lives and classrooms of American's Indians. It was an acknowledged fact that Indian students were not succeeding in the white man's classroom. In 1990, Native Americans had one of the nation's highest rates of illiteracy and high school delinquency. One study classified fully one-third of all Native Americans as educationally handicapped. It is estimated that the average Navaho adult has just five years of formal schooling!

American Indian Movement (AIM) leaders Russell Means (left) and Dennis Banks (seated with vest) celebrate after charges were dismissed in their trial for the occupation of Wounded Knee.

American Indians and their supporters parade in front of the White House.

Despite its good intentions, the Indian Self-Determination Act has yet to reap the full benefits its supporters would like to see. Funding for new schools, teachers, and materials is woefully inadequate, and some critics feel that the Act is just another way for the federal government to avoid providing assistance for Indian education.

Throughout the late 1970s and into the 1980s, Indians continued to stage sit-ins and other protests to call attention to their problems. Today, Indians still have not achieved the equality they seek. In many communities, tribal members do not have access to adequate health care, higher education, or even a decent place to live and work. The life expectancy in some tribes is just forty-five years, the leading cause of death is alcoholism, and Indians have both the highest unemployment rate and the lowest per capita income of any ethnic group in the U.S. Tribe leaders are working hard to correct these problems, even as they strive to preserve traditional culture and language and instill a sense of self-respect based on a time-honored heritage.

There are some hopeful signs. Indian lawyers are fighting for tribal rights in courtrooms across the nation, in greater numbers than ever before. Indian rights campaigns have also been waged in the legislatures, at local, state, and national levels. One such campaign was the crusade to return sacred Indian burial relics and remains of Indian ancestors—now collected in museums and university research departments around the country—to their rightful tribes. The campaign was waged successfully, and in November 1990, President Bush signed into law a bill to protect Indian grave sites in the U.S. and to return remains to the rightful tribes.

Other battles are still being fought. Sports teams around the country continue to use Native American symbols and mascots in discriminatory, demeaning ways. Non-Indian land developers still seek to take over lands and waterways on which Indians have long held traditional hunting and fishing rights.

But the 1990 census showed a marked increase in the number of people identifying themselves as American Indians, indicating a correlating increase in rediscovered roots and ethnic pride. And in December 1990, one hundred years after soldiers of the 7th Cavalry slaughtered hundreds of Sioux men, women, and children at a place called Wounded Knee, descendants of the survivors walked or rode horseback hundreds of miles across the freezing plains of South Dakota to pay homage. The solemn ceremony of purification was the culmination of a "Year of Reconciliation" between whites and Indians of South Dakota.

And so the struggle goes on. Bit by bit, Native Americans are regaining their lost rights—to practice their religions, enforce their laws, educate their children, retrieve their lost lands, and preserve their ancient cultures from extinction. Like other minorities, they continue to work to achieve equal opportunity and justice in a country whose promises of liberty and justice for all has oftentimes rung hollow through the years.

HISPANIC CIVIL RIGHTS

Spanish-speaking peoples constitute the largest non-English-speaking minority in the United States today. And though these people hail from a variety of countries and cultures, on official forms everywhere they are grouped together as "Hispanics." Yet Hispanics are not a homogenous group by any definition. Some can trace their ancestry on U.S. soil as far back as the sixteenth century. Others arrived just last year. Some hail from Mexico, some from Puerto Rico, some from Cuba, some from Central America. Many are farm laborers and unskilled workers; many others are professionals and entrepreneurs. And though they all deserve—and to one degree or another have fought for—civil rights under the United States Constitution, their problems are particular to their original nationalities.

Mexican Americans make up the largest percentage of Hispanics living in the United States and are leaders in the struggle for rights of all Spanish-speaking minorities. Historically, Mexicans were living in what is now the southwestern portion of the United States as early as 1540, when Spanish conquistadors arrived. These people had a proud history that included the spectacular Aztec Empire, which flourished from about 1450 to 1521.

When the Mexican War ended in 1848, the southwestern region became part of the United States, and the Mexicans who lived there became U.S. citizens. These early Mexican Americans learned English, bought farms, and gained a level of acceptability among their Anglo neighbors. The early Mexican Americans remained mostly in the southwestern portion of the country.

Immigration from Mexico to the United States was not widespread before the twentieth century. In 1900, there were no more than 49,000 official Mexican immigrants. The number was difficult to measure because Mexicans disregarded the border between the United States and Mexico and moved back and forth at will. After working for American labor contractors in the Southwest, many Mexican migrants usually earned enough to return to their villages, buy a small farm or business, and live in relative comfort. But a few of the migrant workers settled in the Southwest. They clung to their language and culture. They were mainly poor, illiterate farm workers, quite unlike the older, more established Mexican-American families already in the area. Whites living in the Southwest grew alarmed at the growing Mexican population.

It was not long before southwesterners responded to Mexican migrants with racist Jim Crow laws that maintained segregation of the races. By 1945, there were about 750,000 Mexican Americans living in the United States, mostly concentrated in Arizona, Texas, New Mexico, Southern California, Nevada, and Colorado. By 1980 that number had tripled.

César Chavez, head of the United Farm Workers Union, worked to improve conditions of Mexican Americans.

But an awareness of Mexican Americans as a potentially powerful political group came during the 1960 presidential campaign. "Viva Kennedy" clubs were organized to consolidate the Mexican-American vote for candidate John F. Kennedy, who received 80 percent of their vote. In the Kennedy administration, Raymond Telles, the former mayor of El Paso, Texas, was appointed ambassador to Costa Rica, the first Mexican American to become an ambassador.

People who vote get the attention of politicians. After the 1960 election, people began listening to Mexican-American concerns and demands. A study showed that Mexican Americans were lacking in job skills and education. Low-paying jobs locked them into poor living conditions. Migrant workers moved from farm to farm, earning low wages and working in deplorable conditions. Migrant children hardly had a chance to succeed because educational opportunities were limited.

Cesar Chavez was determined to improve the working conditions of the migrant worker. Chavez, a migrant worker himself, tried to organize the California grape pickers. The wealthy growers blocked his efforts by using age-old tactics of terror, bigotry, and misuse of power. Chavez called for *la huelga*, which means "the strike." Chavez petitioned Americans to help their cause by not buying grapes or products made with grapes. It was a long, bitter struggle, but by the 1970s, grape pickers were allowed to unionize. Afterward, conditions improved greatly.

Education was another major concern among Mexican-Americans. In testimony that was given to the U.S. Commission on Civil Rights in 1966, Dr. Manual Ramz of the Department of Psychology at Rice University said,

> The Mexican-American student is led to believe that he cannot be identified with two cultures at the same time. This is brought about as a result of two conflicting messages. One [of these messages] is given him by his parents, his relatives, other Mexican-American students, who tell him that if he rejects Mexican-American culture, he may be considered a traitor to his ethnic group. The other message comes from teachers, employers, Anglo friends, who tell him that if he doesn't reject the Mexican-American culture then he will be unable to reap the educational and economical benefits that are available in the Anglo society.

Opinions in the Mexican-American community varied. The more militant group of Mexicans called themselves "Chicanos." Their leaders argued, "We do not want to give up the Spanish language, pray to God in English, substitute mashed potatoes for frijoles or junk our piatas . . . Rather than the melting pot, we believe in the heterogeneity of American society, including the give and take with other people of other cultures." There were other Mexican-American leaders who cautioned that their people would forever be "outsiders" as long as they spoke Spanish and clung solely to their culture.

By 1976, many school systems had employed Mexican-American classroom teachers and more Spanish-speaking teachers. There remains, however, a bitter controversy over bilingual education for all Hispanic students. Critics of bilingual education say that the sooner children learn English, the better off they are. Other educators say that a large population of Americans speak Spanish. Why should the only language in America be English? Why cannot children learn both Spanish and English at the same time?

In the 1970s, one-third of all Mexican Americans earned less than did whites or blacks. Equal employment opportunities, education, and fair housing were the main issues that concerned them. Rodolfo Gonzales of Colorado founded the Crusade for Justice in 1965. This organization tried to provide social services and job opportunities for Mexican Americans. Reies Lopez Tijerina of New Mexico and Angel Gutierrez of Texas continued to speak for portions of the Mexican-American population.

By maintaining a strong voting record, they have been able to elect Mexican Americans to public offices locally and nationally. By the 1990s, Mexican Americans had been elected to the U.S. House of Representatives, to the U.S. Senate, as governors of two states, and as mayors of major cities such as San Antonio and Miami. In 1988, Lauro Cavazos was appointed secretary of education— the first Mexican American to hold cabinet rank in the United States.

Puerto Ricans, who are U.S. citizens, are the second-largest Spanish-speaking population in the United States. The greatest number of Puerto-Rican immigrants came to the United States in the 1950s and 1960s, in response to U.S. demand for low-wage, unskilled labor. Some Puerto Ricans settled as far west as Chicago; most, however, settled along the east coast, especially in New York City. Like other minorities, they were and continue to be victims of racial and economic discrimination.

The third-largest Spanish-speaking minority in the United States is Cubans, most of whom live in Florida. When Fidel Castro took over the Cuban government in the late 1950s, nearly 300,000 Cubans fled the country. The vast majority settled in Miami, Florida—just more than 100 miles from Havana. These early Cuban immigrants were, for the most part, ambitious, well-educated, and eager to build successful new lives for themselves in America. It wasn't long before they were earning more, on the average, than non-Hispanic whites in Miami. By 1980, 41 percent of the city's population was Hispanic, making it a truly bilingual, bicultural community.

Migrant workers, many of Hispanic background, move from harvest to harvest often not even earning subsistence wages.

Then, in 1980, the second wave of Cuban immigrants arrived, in what has come to be known as the Mariel exodus. Many of these immigrants had been encouraged to leave Cuba by Fidel Castro, whose government was having trouble supporting all its citizens. A number of them turned out to have social and emotional problems; others were criminals. And the majority, who were healthy male blue-collar workers, lacked the skills and English-speaking abilities to qualify for jobs. Even though Miami's Spanish-speaking population did their best to ease their transition, many of these more recent immigrants found life in their new land difficult. Like other minorities before them, they frequently found themselves the victims of racial and economic discrimination.

The fourth-largest group of Hispanic Americans is those hailing from the countries of war-torn Latin America. Many of these are recent immigrants, desperate to escape the poverty and violence of their homelands. Many are also "undocumented immigrants," or illegal aliens who risk being deported with every move. Of all immigrant groups, Latin Americans have the lowest education and the lowest income, and are frequently viewed with distrust by other Americans.

By the turn of the century, it is estimated that Hispanics will become the largest minority group in the United States. To avoid becoming the largest oppressed group in the United States as well, Hispanic officials (whose numbers tripled from 1973 to 1991) are working hard at the local, state, and federal level to assure equal rights and opportunities for all Spanish-speaking people within America's borders. As with all other minorities, education remains a key issue. The bad news is that Hispanic students have the highest school dropout rate of any ethnic group. The good news is that Hispanic college graduates increased 50 percent during the 1980s. To achieve true racial and economic equality, the first trend will have to be reversed, and the second strongly encouraged.

Joseph Montoya of New Mexico was the first Mexican American to serve in the U.S. Senate.

THE "NEW" MINORITIES

In 1980, more than 6 percent of the American population was foreign born—higher than it had been for more than thirty years. And while immigrants in the early part of the century were overwhelmingly white and European, by 1990 most were Hispanic and Asian from Third World countries—Mexico and Latin American, the Caribbean islands, India, China, the Philippines, Cuba, Vietnam, Thailand, and Cambodia.

Immigration from the Caribbean region began around 1945. West Indians settled along the eastern seaboard and became a part of the black-American community. They were a proud people who took pride in their African heritage. Toussaint-Louverture, a Haitian, was their national hero and role model. He had defeated Napoleon's army on the Caribbean island of the Dominican Republic and had emancipated the slaves. Marked by their industrious nature and strong sense of black pride, West Indians often became educational and political leaders within the black community. By the 1980s, many doctors, lawyers, dentists, educators, and entertainers were West Indian immigrants.

This Haitian married couple arrived in the country illegally in 1981. They were detained in a camp to wait for their deportation hearing.

When Saigon fell to the Communists in 1975, hundreds of thousands of South Vietnamese who had supported the U.S. during the Vietnam War were forced to flee their homeland. Over the next fifteen years, many more followed, from Vietnam and the surrounding countries of Cambodia, Laos, and Thailand. Nearly 40 percent of these refugees settled in concentrated areas in California, where cities like Fresno experienced a 600 percent increase in the number of Asians in their community in a single decade. These refugees from war-torn areas face special problems in trying to put their lives back together in a foreign country. That many of them face discrimination and distrust is just another burden to bear.

Many recent immigrants from Haiti, India, the Philippines, and China came fleeing desperately poor homelands and tyrannical governments. Some sought refuge in America legally; others came as illegal aliens. In many cases, the color of their skin and their low economic status have exposed them to discriminatory practices in employment, housing, and education. And while the myth of the poor, undereducated immigrant persists, the fact is that even the poorest of the "boat people" from Southeast Asia and Haiti had to have saved up the means to pay for the long journey to the United States. Given the opportunity, most could soon become productive citizens of their adopted land.

Much of this recent immigration is credited to the passage of several immigration laws in the past thirty years. The Immigration Act of 1965 loosened restrictions for immigrants, opening the door for basically anyone who could show family members already in the United States, or could demonstrate useful job skills. The Refugee Act of 1980 eased restrictions for those fleeing oppressive or threatening native governments. In 1986, the Immigration Reform and Control Act granted legal status to thousands of illegal aliens already living and working the in United States. And the Immigration Act of 1990 expanded legal immigration even further in an attempt to attract young, educated, skilled immigrants to America's shores.

Some Americans are not pleased with the wave of immigrants that has flooded our shores over the past twenty years. They fear that these new citizens will take away jobs "older" Americans need. They worry about an imagined threat to English and "the American way" by new languages and cultures. But America has always been a melting pot. As we head into the twenty-first century, one in four Americans will be of Hispanic, African, Asian, or American Indian origin. The only real threat to our society is that these nonwhite, non-European Americans will be denied their right to participate fully in the social, economic, and political life of the United States. With luck and hard work, the day will dawn when racial and ethnic differences are valued rather than discarded, stereotyped, or viewed as inferior.

Justice Sandra Day O'Connor was the first woman justice appointed to the Supreme Court.

CONSERVATISM AND CIVIL RIGHTS

Ronald Reagan was first elected to the U.S. presidency in November 1980. In 1984, he was elected for a second term. President Reagan has been called the most popular president in the history of the country. Under his leadership the United States, which had been moving toward more conservative politics, shifted all the way to the Right.

President Reagan campaigned and gained wide support for his conservative policies. He was against the ERA, and he called for the return of prayer in schools and a moratorium on busing. In addition, Reagan believed in less government and more responsibility given to states (states' rights).

Once in office President Reagan confused his opponents by nominating the first woman to the Supreme Court, Justice Sandra Day O'Connor. Justice O'Connor was known for being "tough but fair," so her appointment was applauded by liberals, moderates, and conservatives. O'Connor easily won approval in the Senate.

The appointment of Jeane Kirkpatrick was another unusual move. The president appointed Kirkpatrick to the post of U.S. ambassador to the United Nations, and she was confirmed by the Senate in January 1981. Kirkpatrick was a lifelong Democrat who supported Ronald Reagan's conservative policies, especially his hard-line stand against communism. Kirkpatrick said that her disenchantment with the Democratic party began during the antiwar period.

Black Americans felt excluded and almost alienated by the Reagan administration. Although Reagan's popularity was immense, he received less than a fraction of 1 percent of the black vote in 1984. The president did not meet with black Congress members for four years and did not support a single civil rights issue while in office.

The 1980s have been compared to the 1880s. Advances that blacks made during Reconstruction were lost when Jim Crow legislation was passed. When blacks and other minorities hear slogans such as "Let's go back to the way things used to be," they are understandably concerned. There is an old adage that says, "When people look back it is usually because they do not like where they are and where they are going."

Jeane Kirkpatrick held the post of U.S. ambassador to the United Nations.

GEORGE BUSH AND "EMPOWERMENT"

Ronald Reagan's White House years were marked by steady declines in federal spending for many social and domestic programs, including those designed specifically to assist minority citizens. When George Bush entered the White House in 1989, he showed every sign of carrying on the Reagan tradition. With a skyrocketing federal deficit, budget cuts were a necessity. And domestic programs— designed to help the minorities, women, and children, who generally carry little economic or political clout—were the easiest to trim.

The buzzword from Washington in the 1990s was "empowerment"— letting people manage their own affairs. In theory, empowerment is simple. You give people a hand up, not a handout. Empowerment encourages individual responsibility and is designed to transfer decisions from an inefficient bureaucracy to the people they most affect.

In practice, of course, empowerment isn't nearly so simple. Consider how it may be used to improve a crumbling inner-city school. Decision-making authority is transferred from an overburdened central bureaucracy to the hands of an elected parent-teacher-principal council. These are the people most involved with the school—surely they know best what school improvements are needed. But school moneys are determined by local taxes. A troubled inner-city school is not likely to be located in a neighborhood marked by flourishing businesses and hefty property taxes. Without money, how can even the most dedicated local school council bring about any real improvements?

In truth, empowerment is only part of the story. Self-help *is* an important part of the equation—but so are civil rights enforcement, government assistance, public and private motivation, wise policy decisions, and an effective use of whatever funds are available. To suggest that any one simple strategy can solve complex social problems is to evade the issue.

THE CIVIL RIGHTS ACT OF 1990

In 1989, the Supreme Court passed down a number of rulings that seriously weakened civil rights protections that had been in effect since the early 1970s. Most of these protections had to do with hiring and firing procedures. Concerned about the effects of these judgments, members of Congress introduced the Civil Rights Act of 1990.

Basically, the Civil Rights Act said that employers must be able to give very good reasons for not hiring women and minorities. The Act also made it easier for job applicants and employees to seek legal help when they felt they had been discriminated against.

The Act passed by large majorities in both the House of Representatives and the Senate. But President Bush denounced the Act as a "quota" bill and in August of 1990 vetoed the legislation. In defending his veto (which was strongly supported by big business), President Bush said that the Act would force employers to hire workers according to their race or sex, instead of by merit. Thus, he reasoned, the Act would become a "quota" bill—even though the act's wording made it clear that it did not "require or encourage" quotas. He and his corporate advisors also claimed that the Act would result in "a bonanza" of lawsuits brought against companies who unintentionally didn't hire women and minorities.

President Bush's veto was a major setback for civil rights activists. Supporters felt that the Act would merely have restored rights that had been in effect in the workplace for the eighteen years between 1971 and 1989. During that time, neither quotas nor excessive lawsuits had been a major problem. But the threat of forcing a quota system on employers, and of stripping them of their time-honored American right to hire and fire whom they pleased, proved effective for President Bush.

The real questions raised by the debate over the Civil Rights Act are not easy to answer. Should employers be "forced" to hire minorities if they are not as qualified as white males? Is this sort of affirmative action insulting to women and minorities? Does it encourage racism and sexism by implying that certain members of our society are, in fact, inferior beings who need special favors to succeed? If a minority candidate lacks job qualifications, whose fault is it? Should job standards be lowered—or should greater efforts be made to ensure that all our citizens have equal training and educational opportunities? Wouldn't better education and job training benefit everyone in our society, male or female, black or white?

In 1991, Congress was back at work drafting a new Civil Rights Act. The debate continues.

Forward March

And so the civil rights movement rolls on. It is true that the present is not too bright for a lot of Americans. Inner-city schools and neighborhoods remain largely segregated. Single-parent families with women—often teenaged women—as the heads of households are increasing daily, creating a new underclass. According to one survey, almost one in four black men aged twenty to twenty-nine is in jail, in prison, or on probation or parole; the leading cause of death among young black men is murder.

Unemployment statistics among black, Hispanics, and American Indians are on the rise—as high as 25 percent for urban blacks and Hispanics; up to 80 percent in some Indian tribes—and without a doubt racism is alive and well all over the world. Perhaps the most frightening statistics are those concerning American children. For our children—whatever their race or ethnicity—are our future. If they are uneducated, unfed, and uncared for, they cannot grow up to be the kind of committed, responsible citizens our country will need as we move into the twenty-first century.

Despite parental opposition and other difficulties, the nation's school are gradually becoming integrated.

But even with many setbacks, progress is being made. Dr. Martin Luther King, Jr.'s birthday, like those of Washington and Lincoln, is now a national holiday. It is celebrated on the third Monday in January. It was an American first. The Reverend Jesse Jackson, a black man, ran impressive campaigns in two Democratic presidential primaries in the 1980s. Henry Cisneros, a Mexican-American mayor of San Antonio, was the first Hispanic ever considered for the office of Vice-President of the United States, in Walter Mondale's 1984 presidential campaign. In the end, Mondale chose Geraldine Ferraro to be his running mate—a woman of Italian descent. This was another first for our country.

The struggle goes on each day in courts, Congress, schools, churches, businesses, even in your home. Progress is a slow journey—often one step forward and two backward, but always moving. And no matter how much ground is lost, America will never go back to the way things were a century ago, or even three decades ago. Today, blacks—and women and Indians and Hispanics and Asians—can vote. They can organize to bring about the changes

Reverend Jesse Jackson debates with two other presidential hopefuls, former Vice President Walter Mondale and Senator Gary Hart.

necessary to insure true racial harmony in America.

The black revolution was the first and arguably the most important of our civil rights movements. It inspired other minorities to work together to demand their own civil rights. Often these other minorities used tactics they learned from black leaders such as Martin Luther King, Jr., to bring their demands to the public eye. And though each group had its own needs clearly in mind, they shared many of the same goals and values—to achieve true economic, political, and social equality. White, black, red, yellow, and brown people are, as they have always been, the hope of America and the future of democracy. It will take the strength, courage, and devotion of each citizen to keep freedom and justice a reality for all Americans, regardless of race, color, age, sex, religion, and national origin. Until that happens, the civil rights movement will not—cannot—end.

An American marine plays with two Vietnamese children.

Cameos

THE *MIRANDA* RULING

In 1966, the Supreme Court ruled that accused criminals had the right to remain silent and to have a lawyer and that it is the duty and responsibility of the arresting officer to make sure that the person arrested understands his rights.

Critics of the *Miranda* ruling claim that it favors the criminal and that it hinders law enforcers from doing their job. Supporters argue that the law helps to protect the innocent who were often abused by the law.

JAPANESE REPARATION

The Japanese bombing of Pearl Harbor on December 7, 1941, marked the beginning of a long and devastating war between Japan and the United States. But not all of the Japanese victims of World War II lived in Japan. Thousands of Japanese Americans living up and down the Pacific Coast of the United States were also affected.

To a nation at war, these Japanese Americans, many of whose families had lived in the United States for generations, suddenly became "the enemy." Their homes and property were seized, and they themselves—men, women, and children—were "relocated" into internment camps, where they lived as virtual prisoners for the duration of the war. Even after the war, many Japanese Americans were viewed with distrust and

An aerial view of the Japanese relocation center at Minidoka, Idaho.

The day after their arrival at the Manzanar internment camp these Japanese men were put to work clearing land for spring planting.

blatantly discriminated against. Most never recovered their lost homes or property. They were forced to begin their lives again, without government assistance of any sort.

Finally, in October 1990, nine elderly men and women became the first Japanese Americans to receive reparation payments from the United States for their relocation and internment during World War II. The payments, for $20,000 each, were just a fraction of the more than $1.25 billion allocated by Congress in 1988 for victims of the internment. In handing out the payments, Attorney General Dick Thornburgh apologized for one of the United States' most shameful actions of this century:

> Your struggle for redress and the events that led to today are the finest example of what our country is about and of what we have pledged to protect and defend. Your efforts have strengthened the nation's Constitution by reaffirming the inalienability of our civil rights.

> We enjoy a precious system of government that is unsurpassed by any in the world. Even when that system failed you, you never lost your faith in it. On the contrary, you believed that through that system you could achieve the justice which you have been denied. By finally admitting a wrong, a nation does not destroy its integrity but, rather, reinforces the sincerity of its commitment to the Constitution and hence to its people.

> In forcing us to re-examine our history, you have made us only stronger and more proud. For that, all Americans are indebted to you. I am not unmindful of the historic role this Department of Justice played in the internment. It is somehow entirely fitting that it is here we now celebrate redress.

GAY AND LESBIAN RIGHTS

When Illinois adopted the Model Legal Code of the American Law Institute in 1961, it became the first state to decriminalize homosexuality between consenting adults in private. Today, some thirty years later, homosexuality remains one of the most controversial topics in contemporary American society. Whether for religious or moral reasons, many Americans are uncomfortable with, or intolerant of, the idea of gay and lesbian lifestyles. As a result, like other minority groups, homosexuals have been subject to a multitude of violations to their basic civil rights as Americans.

As the gay rights movement gained momentum in the 1960s, gay men and lesbians drew up a comprehensive list of "wants." These included such basics as:

- no discrimination in employment, housing, education, and health care

- custody and visitation rights for gay parents

- recognition of the legal, social, and financial rights of two people of the same sex living together as a couple

- the right to adopt children

- the declassification of homosexuality as mental illness

The AIDS health crisis of the 1980s focused a great deal of negative publicity on homosexuals, especially on the gay men who were the disease's main victims. Instead of sympathy, AIDS sufferers were subjected to hostility, fear, and a mostly uninterested medical community. As more became known about the disease, public opinion calmed down somewhat, but many AIDS sufferers are still subjected to discrimination by employers, insurance companies, and even the health care profession. While gay rights activists have become more political and more organized in recent years, and have made some strides in regaining their civil rights, the battle is by no means won yet.

Like other minority groups before them, persons suffering from AIDS found it necessary to take their cause into the streets to bring the health crisis to the attention of America.

Allan Bakke (left) at his graduation from the University of California. Two members (right) of the National Socialist Party of America, Michael Kelly and Frank Collins, in front of Rockwell Hall, the Nazi headquarters in Chicago.

Rights of Another Kind

THE BAKKE DECISION

Allan Bakke was refused admission to the University of California at Davis Medical School. Although Bakke had an excellent academic record, other less qualified applicants were admitted to increase the school's minority enrollment. He sued and won. The U.S. Supreme Court ruled in 1978 that Bakke had been a victim of "reverse discrimination," so he was admitted to the school.

THE SKOKIE CASE

A neo-Nazi group planned to stage a march through the predominantly Jewish neighborhood of Skokie, Illinois. Many German concentration camp survivors lived in this suburb of Chicago. Naturally, the citizens protested against such a march, saying that it was an abominable thing to do. Many people outside the Jewish community agreed. Imagine the Klan marching in Harlem! There were threats of violence from militant Jewish groups who promised to stop the march by force if the courts did not stop it.

After long and heated court battles, the courts ruled for the neo-Nazis. They were granted a march permit, but they canceled the march.

The same court orders that granted Martin Luther King, Jr.'s march in Alabama gave the neo-Nazis the same right to hold a march in Illinois. In a true democracy, even the Ku Klux Klan, the Nazis, and other racist organizations have rights. They are rights of another kind.

Justice Thurgood Marshall   *Lieutenant Colonel Hazel W. Johnson*

MINORITY FIRSTS

Herbert Y. Choy was an Asian American who served as the attorney general of Hawaii in 1957–58, before Hawaii was a state. President Nixon appointed Mr. Choy to the U.S. Court of Appeals. Judge Choy was the first person of Asian ancestry to serve as a federal judge.

Hazel W. Johnson was the first black brigadier general in the United States Army Nurse Corps. General Benjamin O. Davis, Sr., was the first black to obtain the rank of general in the U.S. Army during Roosevelt's administration, and his son, General Benjamin D. Davis, Jr., was the first black to obtain the rank of general in the U.S. Air Force. General Colin L. Powell was the first black to be named Chairman of the Joint Chiefs of Staff.

Thurgood Marshall was an outstanding lawyer for the NAACP and the first black to be appointed to the Supreme Court. He was appointed by President Lyndon B. Johnson.

L. Douglas Wilder was the first black governor in the United States. He was elected governor of Virginia in 1990.

Sharon Pratt Dixon was the first black woman mayor of a major U.S. city. She was elected mayor of Washington, D.C., in November 1990.

B'NAI B'RITH

The term "B'nai B'rith" means "sons of the Covenant." B'nai B'rith is the oldest Jewish organization in the United States, dating back to 1843. Today, it has worldwide membership with over a half million members.

B'nai B'rith is a service organization whose members follow the precepts of love and brotherhood. An auxiliary group, the Hillel Foundation, is located on some college campuses. In 1913, the Anti-Defamation League was founded to combat anti-Semitism.

In Marietta, Georgia, Leo Frank, a twenty-nine-year-old Jewish superintendent of a pencil factory, was accused of raping and killing a thirteen-year-old white girl. He was tried and convicted of the crime and sentenced to life in prison. A mob stormed the jail and lynched Frank in the square. Afterward, Georgia Klan activity against Jews spread, and the newly formed Anti-Defamation League fought to defend the rights of Jewish Americans—much like the NAACP fights for the rights of blacks.

In 1986, Leo Frank's name was cleared when the state of Georgia pardoned him. An eighty-five-year-old witness came forth with evidence that cleared Frank.

PRAYER IN SCHOOL

Two Supreme Court decisions in 1962 and 1963 continue to be the most controversial of all civil rights legislation. The Supreme Court ruled that school prayer and Bible reading were unconstitutional. In the Justices' opinions, public schools were paid for by local, state, and federal funds. Since the United States has a strict division between church and state, it was ruled unconstitutional for religion to be "used" in school.

Should there be prayer in school? If so, when? Where? How will it be conducted? Will prayers be Catholic, Protestant, Jewish, Moslem, Hindu, or pagan? What about those who do not want to pray? What will happen to them? What rights does the individual have regarding prayer? These and other questions are being asked by both sides in the controversy. What do you think?

STUDENTS FOR A DEMOCRATIC SOCIETY (SDS)

By the late 1960s, the organization called Students for a Democratic Society (SDS) was active on college campuses. It had been started in June 1962 by forty-five young undergraduate students, who had met at a camp at Port Huron, Michigan. Tom Hayden, who was then a student at the University of Michigan, was a founder and also helped draft the organization's goals and purpose. The group cited two destructive forces that threatened the American public: racism and the threat of nuclear war. Later, the SDS would advocate "violence as a catalyst for change." But Hayden and the early founders rejected that concept.

Tom Hayden

EXTREMISM

Extremism during the late 1960s and early 1970s is represented in two organizations: The John Birch Society and the Weathermen.

The John Birch Society is an ultraconservative organization that strives to combat communism. It was started in Belmont, Massachusetts, in 1958. Throughout its history, the John Birch Society has opposed the United Nations, foreign aid, the North Atlantic Treaty Organization (NATO), and any contact with the Soviet Union. The organization is still in existence and has about ninety thousand members.

The Weathermen was the radical outgrowth of the Students for a Democratic Society (SDS). The SDS radically opposed the Vietnam War and staged demonstrations and protests against U.S. involvement there. In 1969, a small group within the SDS felt that the organization was not radical enough and left to form the Weathermen. The Weathermen advocated violence to achieve their goals and were believed to be responsible for bombings in factories that manufactured weapons used in Vietnam.

MORRIS DEES AND "HATE" CRIMES

In October 1990, lawyer Morris Dees won a $12.5 million verdict against members of the national racist organization, White Aryan Resistance, for their brutal murder of a twenty-seven-year-old Ethiopian man in Portland, Oregon. Dees's Alabama-based Southern Poverty Law Center specializes in suing hate groups; in 1987, Dees won a $7 million lawsuit against the United Klan of America for shooting and hanging a black youth. The 1987 lawsuit bankrupted the admittedly racist Klan, and Dees hopes to accomplish the same aim with the White Aryan Resistance. Of his victories, Dees says, "The jury has spoken loud and clear that in this country the First Amendment guarantees the right to hate people and say what you want, but not the right to hurt people."

CESAR CHAVEZ

Born in 1927 into a poor Mexican-American family, Cesar Chavez understood the plight of the migrant workers firsthand. He saw his fellow workers laboring long hours for low pay and living in unsanitary housing.

Chavez organized the National Farm Workers Association, the first union to represent migrant farm laborers. Chavez was a poor man, but he fought to keep the union alive, often having to beg for food to keep his family going. He was discouraged by his own people, mocked by the peaceful grape growers, and ignored by the apathetic public.

Cesar Chavez would not give up. He persisted, following in the footsteps of Martin Luther King, Jr., and Mahatma Gandhi. He used nonviolent protests to achieve reform. Chavez devoted his life and endured many hardships to help farm workers gain their economic rights.

MAYA ANGELOU

Maya Angelou is a black American poet who attended the Women's Conference in November 1977. This is an excerpt from her speech "To Form a More Perfect Union":

We American women view our history with equanimity. We allow the positive achievement to inspire us and the negative omissions to teach us.

We promise to accept nothing less than justice for every woman.

We pledge to work unsparingly to bring fair play to every public arena, to encourage honorable behavior in each private home.

We promise to develop courage that we may learn from our colleagues and patience that we may attack our opponent.

Because we are women, we make these promises.

CORETTA SCOTT KING

Coretta Scott King is the widow of Dr. Martin Luther King, Jr. After her husband's death, she helped to start, and now serves as the president of, the Martin Luther King, Jr., Center for Social Change in Atlanta, Georgia. She also led the campaign to make Dr. King's birthday a national holiday. Mrs. King is a strong supporter of women's and children's rights.

JAMES BALDWIN

It would be impossible to write anything about the civil rights movement in America and not give special attention to novelist, essayist, and lecturer James Baldwin. In his two collections of essays, *Nobody Knows My Name* (1961) and *The Fire Next Time* (1964), Baldwin speaks out against racism and discrimination in America.

In October 1963, weeks after the Birmingham church bombing, Baldwin spoke to Harlem teachers. This is an excerpt from his "The Negro Child—His Self-Image."

It is inconceivable that a sovereign people should continue, as we do so abjectly, to say, "I can't do anything about it. It's the government." The government is the creation of the people. It is responsible to the people. And the people are responsible for it. No American has the right to allow the present government to say, when Negro children are being bombed and hosed and shot and beaten all over the Deep South, that there is nothing we can do about it. There must have been a day in this country's life when the bombing of four children in Sunday School would have created a public uproar and endangered the life of Governor Wallace. It happened here, and there was no uproar.

As both a black man and a gay man, James Baldwin understood the importance of civil rights and what life without them was like.

Elijah Muhammad   Louis Farrakan

ELIJAH MUHAMMAD AND THE NATION OF ISLAM

Elijah Poole was born in 1897 in Sandersville, Georgia. As a child he worked in the fields and in a sawmill. Like many southerners, he left the South in 1923 and worked for a while at the Chevrolet automobile plant in Detroit. In 1930, Elijah Poole met Master W.D. Far, who taught him the principles on which he was to build the National Islam. The first thing was to discard the slàvemaster's last name. Elijah Poole changed his name to Elijah Muhammad, and he built Temple No. 1 in Chicago in 1932. Today, there are Nation of Islam temples all over the country. (The Nation of Islam is not to be confused with the Muslim religion, although they use similar worship terms.)

The "Black Muslims," as they are frequently called by nonmembers, began a self-help program that was appealing to many young blacks who wanted to identify positively with something progressive. Under the strict directorship of Elijah Muhammad, members are not permitted to use drugs or alcohol. The Nation of Islam opened restaurants, supermarkets, construction companies, clothing stores, a meat processing plant, farms, and orchards.

After Elijah Muhammad died, Louis Farrakan became the spiritual leader and the primary spokesman for the Nation of Islam.

ROY WILKINS

Roy Wilkins was born in St. Louis in 1901. After graduation from the University of Minnesota, he was the managing editor of a weekly newspaper in Kansas City.

In 1931, Wilkins joined the national NAACP staff and served as assistant secretary and editor of *Crisis* from 1934 to 1949. During the 1960s, Wilkins was a prominent leader in the civil rights movement as the national executive director of the NAACP. Wilkins was one of the organizers of the march on Washington in 1963. This is an excerpt from the speech he gave:

Just by your presence here today we have spoken loudly and eloquently to our legislature. When we return home, keep up the speaking by letters and telegrams and telephone and, wherever possible, by personal visit. Remember that this has been a long fight. We were reminded of it by the news of the death yesterday in Africa of Dr. W.E.B. DuBois. Now, regardless of the fact that in his later years Dr. DuBois chose another path, it is incontrovertible that at the dawn of the twentieth century his was the voice that was calling to you to gather here today in this cause. If you want to read something that applies to 1963 go back and get a volume of *The Souls of Black Folk* by DuBois published in 1903.

JESSE JACKSON

Jesse Jackson has been described as charismatic, outspoken, flamboyant, vain, compassionate, and a perpetual troublemaker. Since the 1960s, he has been an active civil rights leader and a controversial figure in American politics. His constituents are the poor and the underprivileged.

Just before his death, Martin Luther King, Jr., appointed Jackson to run the SCLC's Operation Breadbasket, which was headquartered in Chicago. Several years later, Jackson broke with the SCLC and began Operation PUSH in 1971.

Operation PUSH has targeted four goals: voter registration, economic development among blacks and other minorities, education of youths, and international development. Jackson's antidrug campaign reaches out to youths all over the country. "Say no to drugs—say yes to life." He also works to increase voter registration and to have better informed voters. For these programs he has been commended. But sometimes Jackson's views are unpopular. He has been sharply criticized for his views on the Middle East, the military budget, and domestic cutbacks in social programs.

Since 1980, Jackson has been recognized as an international human rights leader. "I am not a black leader," said Jackson in a June 1981 interview with *Ebony* magazine. "I am a moral leader who happens to be Black… . Black is not used by the media to describe my color; my color is self-evident. In this context, Black is used to define the domain of my leadership, which they want to limit. Whites want us to lead the ghetto while they lead the world. I argue that I am a human rights and moral leader who should not be denied the opportunity to lead whoever will follow my ideas, and that my ideas should be judged in the universe of ideas."

During the 1984 Democratic presidential primaries, Jackson represented what he called the Rainbow Coalition, which included all minorities, women, the "new poor," farmers, and children. Jackson ran an impressive campaign, but during the campaign, he privately called New York City "Hymietown," which is a racial slur against Jews. Jews were outraged when the comment was made public by a reporter who had overheard the conversation. The incident seriously jeopardized Jackson's campaign and caused many to question his integrity. At the 1984 Democratic convention in San Francisco, Jackson apologized for his statement saying that it was a mistake of the head, and not of the heart.

In 1988, Jackson ran an even stronger race for the Democratic nomination for president. This time, he added thousands of white votes to his solid black support base. Though he did not win the nomination, he brought the idea of a black president closer to the American consciousness.

Since 1988, Jackson has continued his right for human rights and minority political power on both a national and international level.

WHITNEY YOUNG

During the peak of the civil rights movement in the 1960s, Whitney Young was the executive director of the Urban League. Before that, he had been a dean at the Atlanta University School of Social Work.

He served on a number of presidential committees in the Kennedy and Johnson administrations, such as Youth Employment; Equal Opportunity in the Armed Forces; the National Commission on Technology, Automation, and Economic Progress; and the National Advisory Council on Economic Opportunity. He also helped to plan the march on Washington in 1963.

In 1964, Young addressed the National Conference of the Urban League. This is an excerpt from that speech:

The Negro citizen and the Urban League are challenged today as never before—to help citizens help themselves in the use of the tools and resources of existing institutions—to take direct action and to participate fully in the life of their communities. As I said at the March on Washington a year ago, it is not enough to march on picket lines; our citizens must also march beyond protest to *participate*. We must march to PTA meetings, to libraries, to vocational and apprentice training courses. We must march to decision-making meetings on town zoning, urban renewal, health, welfare, and education. These are the sensitive points in which our participation will determine how our children and grandchildren will live.

PRESIDENT JAMES (JIMMY) CARTER AND HUMAN RIGHTS

Jimmy Carter, the thirty-ninth president of the United States, was elected by 51 percent of the popular vote in 1976. Carter was a Georgian and the first president elected from the Deep South since the Civil War. (Lyndon Johnson was from Texas, which is considered a Western state.) Also, Carter was supported by a large percentage of the minority vote.

Carter served only one term (1976-80), but he will be most remembered and respected for his worldwide human rights position. He spoke out against repressive governments that denied their citizens basic human rights, for example, the Soviets' oppression of Russian Jews. Carter's focus on human rights made Americans more aware of South Africa's apartheid system, Haiti's cruel dictatorship, and the corrupt Marcos regime in the Philippines, which has since been replaced by the democratic government of President Corazon Aquino. Human rights groups, many of which were established during the Carter administration, continue to fight for the rights of mankind all over the world. Carter himself also continues to work for disadvantaged and handicapped people around the world, via his private charity, Global 2000, and other organizations.

RALPH ABERNATHY

Ralph Abernathy was Martin Luther King, Jr.'s friend and closest adviser. Their friendship began in 1954, when both men were pastors of churches in Montgomery, Alabama.

Abernathy became a principal leader in the contemporary civil rights movement, beginning with the Montgomery bus boycott. Abernathy marched beside King in countless demonstrations and endured many hardships with his friend. When Dr. King's associates criticized King for speaking against the Vietnam War, Abernathy remained loyal to him.

After King's death Abernathy became president of the SCLC and conducted the poor people's march on Washington that Dr. King had planned during the summer of 1968.

ANDREW YOUNG

Andrew (Andy) Young was born March 12, 1932, in New Orleans, Louisiana. He was a 1951 graduate of Howard University in Washington, D.C., and was ordained a Congregationalist minister. During the 1960s, Young worked for the SCLC, coordinating marches and demonstrations. After King's death, Young turned to politics.

He represented Georgia's 5th District in the U.S. House of Representatives from 1972 to 1976. He was the first black congressman from Georgia since Reconstruction.

During the Carter administration, Andrew Young was the U.S. ambassador to the United Nations. He was criticized for his candid and, often, "undiplomatic" language. He was greatly admired by African nations, however, and he helped to strengthen relations between moderate African countries and the United States.

In 1979, Ambassador Young met secretly with a member of the Palestine Liberation Organization (PLO). Since the PLO was considered a terrorist organization that the United States publicly denounced, Young resigned. He returned to Georgia, where he was elected mayor of Atlanta in 1981. He served two terms, leaving office in 1989 to mount an unsuccessful bid for Georgia's governorship in 1990. Now a private citizen, Andrew Young is still an active voice in the human rights movement.

ALEX HALEY'S *ROOTS*

Alex Haley was down to eighteen cents and two cans of sardines, but he finished writing his book *Roots: The Saga of an American Family,* which gave millions of Americans another real picture of slavery. The story, which is historical fiction based on his family history, began when Alex traced his heritage back to an African warrior named Kunte Kinte. The book was a best-seller, and the television production which first aired in 1977 won numerous awards. Haley's book sparked interest in family history, reunions, genealogy, and, again, racial pride. Haley also wrote numerous articles and assisted the author in the well-known autobiography of Malcolm X.

A century earlier, before the Civil War, Harriet Beecher Stowe wrote *Uncle Tom's Cabin.* Her portrait of slavery helped to rally antislavery supporters.

THE CIVIL RIGHTS COMMISSION

As part of the Civil Rights Act of 1957, the Civil Rights Commission, an independent advisory agency attached to the executive branch of the government, was established. The commission consisted of six members—not more that three from each political party could serve at the same time. Commissioners were appointed by the president and approved by the Senate. From the commissioners, a chairman and co-chairman were appointed to serve indefinite terms.

The duties of the commission were spelled out in Section 104 of the Civil Rights Act of 1957.

    (a) The Commission shall—

(1) investigate allegations in writing under oath…that certain citizens of the United States are being deprived of their right to vote and have that vote counted by reason of their color, race, religion, or national origin…

(2) study and collect information concerning legal developments constituting a denial of equal protection of the laws under the Constitution…

(3) appraise the laws and policies of the Federal Government with respect to equal protection of the laws under the Constitution.

The Civil Rights Acts of 1960 and 1964 strengthened the commission's responsibilities and broadened its authority.

FATHER THEODORE MARTIN HESBURGH

Theodore Martin Hesburgh, a Catholic priest, was one of the first members of the Civil Rights Commission in 1958. He served as the chairman from 1969 to 1972, when he was asked to resign by President Nixon.

Father Hesburgh was an outspoken critic of the Nixon administration's handling of minority housing, education, and employment. Father Hesburgh's strongest attack was against President Nixon's anti-busing position. At the beginning of Nixon's second term in 1972, Father Hesburgh was asked to resign his post as chairman of the Civil Rights Commission. Black leaders interpreted the forced resignation of Father Hesburgh as a slap in the face of civil rights.

Theodore Hesburgh was the president of Notre Dame University from 1952 to 1987. He continues to work for civil rights causes, especially in the area of education. In an interview with the Catholic Standard and Times in August 1968, Father Hesburgh responded to a question on civil rights with:

Americans don't like to remember this, but we had apartheid as bad as South Africa up until 1964…but we changed all that…Today, I have the feeling that—and I want to say this carefully—I think the fervor has gone out of the civil rights movement…I think many in the government and past governments have pedaled backward…We still have a long way to go for justice and equality and equal opportunity for all people in America, and this is not the time to rest on the oars.

PRESIDENTS FROM 1961 TO THE PRESENT

John F. Kennedy	1961-1963
Lyndon B. Johnson	1963-1969
Richard M. Nixon	1969-1974
Gerald R. Ford	1974-1977
James E. Carter, Jr.	1977-1981
Ronald W. Reagan	1981-1989
George Bush	1989-

JOHN F.KENNEDY

LYNDON B. JOHNSON

RICHARD M. NIXON

GERALD R. FORD

JAMES E. CARTER, JR.

RONALD W. REAGAN

GEORGE BUSH

BIBLIOGRAPHY

Adams, Russell L. *Great Negroes Past and Present*, Third Edition. New York: Afro-Am Publishing Company, 1976.

Adler, Mortimer J. gen. ed. *The Negro in American History*. Chicago: Encyclopaedia Britannica Educational Corporation, 1969.

Anderson, Lydia. *Immigration*. New York: Franklin Watts Inc., 1981

Berry, Mary Frances and Blassingame, John W. *Long Memory, The Black Experience in America*. New York: Oxford University Press, 1982.

Bird, Caroline. *What Women Want*. New York: Simon and Schuster Publishers, 1979.

Bettmann, Otto L. *The Bettmann Archive Picture History of the World*. New York: Random House, 1978.

Bontemps, Arna, ed. *American Negro Poetry*. New York: Hill and Wang, 1963.

Broderick, Francis L. *W. E. B. DuBois*. Stanford: Stanford University Press, 1969.

Brown, Richard C., Robinson, Wilhelmena S. and Cunningham, John T. *Let Freedom Ring, A U.S. History*. Morristown, New Jersey: Silver Burdett Company, 1977.

Chambers, Bradford. *Chronicles of Negro Protest*. New York: Parents Magazine Press, 1968.

Cooke, Alistair. *Alistair Cooke's America*. New York: Alfred A. Knopf, 1973.

Corbin, Carole Lynn. *The Right to Vote*. New York: Franklin Watts Inc., 1985.

Donovan, Hedley. *The Great Chiefs*. Alexandria, Virginia: Time-Life Books, Inc., 1975.

Foner, Eric. *America's Black Past*. New York: Harper and Row Publishers, 1970.

Franklin, John Hope. *Racial Equality in America*. Chicago: The University of Chicago Press, 1976.

Freehling, William W. *Willie Lee Rose: Slavery and Freedom*. New York: Oxford University Press, 1982.

Freidman, Leon. *The Civil Rights Reader*. New York: Walker and Company, 1967.

Goode, Stephen. *The New Federalism: States Rights in American History*. New York: Franklin Watts Inc., 1983.

Hale, Frank W., Jr. *The Cry for Freedom*. San Diego: A.S. Barnes and Company, Inc., 1969.

Hand, Learned. *The Bill of Rights*. Cambridge: Harvard University Press, 1958.

Hansberry, Lorraine. *The Movement—Documentary of a Struggle for Equality*. New York: Simon and Schuster Publishers, 1964.

Harding, Vincent. *There is a River—The Black Struggle for Freedom in America*. New York: Harcourt Brace Jovanovich, Publishers, 1981.

Haskins, James. *Revolutionaries: Agents of Change*. New York: J. P. Lippincott Publishers, 1971.

——————. *The Life and Death of Martin Luther King, Jr*. New York: Lothrop, Lee & Shepard Company, 1977.

——————. *The Statue of Liberty*. Minneapolis: Lerner Publications, 1986.

Herbers, John. *The Lost Priority: What Happened to the Civil Rights Movement in America?* New York: Funk and Wagnalls, 1970.

Hersch, Jeanne. *Birthright of Man*. New York: UNESCO, 1969.

Hughes, Langston, Meltzer, Milton and Lincoln, C. Eric. *A Pictorial History of Black Americans*, Fourth Edition. New York: Crown Publishers, Inc., 1983.

Humphrey, Hubert H. *Beyond Civil Rights*. New York: Random House, 1968.

Ianniello, Lynne. *Milestones Along the March*. New York: Frederick Praeger Publishers, 1965.

Killian, Lewis M. *The Impossible Revolution? Black Power and the American Dream*. New York: Random House Publishers, 1968.

King, Martin Luther, Jr. *Stride Toward Freedom*. New York: Harper & Row Publishers, 1958.

Konvitz, Milton R. *A Century of Civil Rights*. New York: Columbia University Press, 1961.

Levitan, Sar A, Johnson, William B. and Taggart, Robert. *Minorities in the United States*. Washington, D.C.: Public Press, 1975.

Luce, Henry, ed. *Time Capsule/1939*. New York: Time-Life Books, Inc., 1968.

McClellan, Grant S. *Civil Rights*. New York: H. W. Wilson Company, 1964.

McKissack, Patricia. *Martin Luther King, Jr*. Chicago: Childrens Press, 1984.

Meier, August and Rudwick, Elliot. *From Plantation to Ghetto*, Third Edition. New York: Hill and Wang Publishers, 1976.

Meltzer, Milton. *The Human Rights Book*. New York: Farrar, Straus, Giroux Publishers, 1979.

Miller, Major Donald L. *Black Americans in the Armed Forces*. New York: Franklin Watts Inc., 1969.

Morris, Richard B. *Encyclopedia of American History*. New York: Harper and Row Publishers, 1961.

Mowry, George E. and Brownell, Blaine A. *The Urban Nation 1920-1980*. New York: Hill and Wang Publishers, 1981.

Oates, Stephen. *Let the Trumpet Sound—The Life of Martin Luther King, Jr*. New York: Harper and Row Publishers, 1982.

Sandburg, Carl. *Abraham Lincoln: The War Years*. New York: Harcourt, Brace & Company, 1939.

Schlesinger, Arthur M., Jr., gen. ed. *The Almanac of American History*. New York: G. P. Putnam and Sons, 1983.

——————. *History of American Presidential Elections—1789-1968*, Volume Two. New York: Chelsea House Publishers, 1971.

Schwartz, Bernard. *The Great Rights of Mankind*. New York: Oxford University Press, 1977.

Sitkoff, Harvard. *The Struggle for Black Equality*. New York: Hill and Wang Publishers, 1981.

Snyder, Gerald S. *Human Rights*. New York: Franklin Watts Inc., 1980.

Sowell, Thomas. *Ethnic America—A History*. New York: Basic Books, Inc., 1981

Sterling, Dorothy. *We Are Your Sisters*. New York: W.W. Norton, 1984.

Young, Whitney. *To Be Equal*. New York: McGraw-Hill Book Company, 1964.

Zinn, Howard. *SNCC: The New Abolitionists*. Boston, Beacon Press, 1964.

ACKNOWLEDGMENTS

Page 20: Excerpt from *Abraham Lincoln: The War Years*, Volume One, by Carl Sandburg. © copyright, 1939, by Harcourt, Brace and Company, Inc. Reprinted by permission of Harcourt Brace Jovanovich, Inc.

Pages 21, 44, 53, 76, 78, 109, 134-135: Excerpts from *The Negro in American History, Volume II, A Taste of Freedom: 1854-1927.* Copyright © 1969 by Encyclopaedia Britannica Educational Corporation. Reprinted by permission of Encyclopaedia Britannica, Inc.

Pages 31, 33, 34, 39, 52: Excerpts from *A Century of Civil Rights* by Milton R. Konvitz. Copyright © 1961 by Columbia University Press. Reprinted by permission.

Pages 38-39, 97: Excerpts from *History of American Presidential Elections 1789-1968* edited by Arthur M. Schlesinger, jr. Copyright © 1971 by Chelsea House Publishers. Reprinted by permission.

Pages 40, 41, 202: Excerpts from *The Rights to Vote* by Carole Lynn Corbin. Copyright © 1985 by Carole Lynn Corbin, published by Franklin Watts.

Pages 50, 59, 79, 80, 81, 82, 126, 130, 155, 235, 252: Excerpts from *Chronicles of Negro Protest* compiled and edited by Bradford Chambers. Copyright © 1968 by Bradford Chambers. Reprinted by permission of Parents Magazine Press, a division of Gruner & Jahr, USA, Publishing.

Pages 51, 283, 287, 288: Excerpts from *Let Freedom Ring, A U.S. History* by Richard C. Brown, Wilhelmena S. Robinson, and John T. Cunningham. © 1977 by Silver Burdett Company.

Page 71: Excerpt from *Immigration* by Lydia Anderson. Copyright © 1981 by Lydia Anderson. Published by Franklin Watts.

Page 94: "Booker T. and W.E.B." by Dudley Randall. Reprinted by permission of Dudley Randall.

Page 95: "Sympathy" by Paul Laurence Dunbar from *The Complete Poems of Paul Laurence Dunbar*, by Paul Laurence Dunbar. Published by Dodd, Mead & Company, Inc., New York, New York, copyright © 1913. Reprinted with permission.

Page 108: Excerpt from *Racial Equality in America* by John Hope Franklin. © 1976 by The University of Chicago. All rights reserved. Published 1976. Printed in the United States of America.

Page 119: Excerpt from *Alistair Cooke's America* by Alistair Cooke. Copyright © 1973 by Alistair Cooke. Reprinted by permission of Alfred A. Knopf, Inc.

Pages 132, 133, 177: Excerpts from *Long Memory* by Mary Frances Berry and John W. Blassingame. Copyright © 1982 by Oxford University Press, Inc.

Pages 137, 165: Excerpt from *The Other American Revolution* by Vincent Harding. Copyright © 1980 by The Regents of the University of California and the Institute of the Black World. Reprinted with permission.

Page 142: "I, Too" by Langston Hughes from *Selected Poems of Langston Hughes*. © 1926 by Alfred A. Knopf, Inc., renewed, 1954 by Langston Hughes. Reprinted by permission.

Page 147: Excerpt from *Franklin Delano Roosevelt: 1882-1945*, edited by Howard F. Beemer. © copyright 1971 by Oceana Publications, Inc. Reprinted by permission of Oceana Publications, Inc., Dobbs Ferry, New York.

Pages 156, 157: Excerpts from *Ethnic America: A History* by Thomas Sowell. Copyright © 1981 by Basic Books, Inc. Reprinted by permission of the publisher.

INDEX

Page numbers that appear in boldface type indicate illustrations.

PHOTO ACKNOWLEDGMENTS

AP/Wide World Photos: Covers (left bottom back cover and right bottom front cover); H. Armstrong Roberts: Cover (center top back cover); North Wind Picture Archives: Cover (left bottom front cover); SuperStock International, Inc.: Cover (right bottom back cover); UPI/Bettmann Newsphotos: Covers (left and right top and center, back cover, left and right top and center, front cover); Historical Pictures Service: 12; AP/Wide World Photos: 14; Historical Pictures Service: 16, 17, 19, 20; H. Armstrong Roberts: 23, 24; North Wind Picture Archives: 25; H. Armstrong Roberts: 26; North Wind Picture Archives: 27; H. Armstrong Roberts: 28; North Wind Picture Archives: 30; U.S. Bureau of Printing and Engraving: 31; Historical Pictures Service: 32, 33, 35, 36; H. Armstrong Roberts: 38; Historical Pictures Service: 39; Reproduced from the collection of the Library of Congress: 41 (left); North Wind Picture Archives: 41 (right); Historical Pictures Service: 43; North Wind Picture Archives: 45, 47 (top); Historical Pictures Service: 47 (bottom); North Wind Picture Archives: 48; H. Armstrong Roberts: 49; North Wind Picture Archives: 50; Historical Pictures Service: 51 (2 photos); North Wind Picture Archives: 53; Historical Pictures Service: 54 (2 photos), 56, 58; AP/Wide World Photos 60; North Wind Picture Archives: 61; Historical Pictures Service: 64, 66; North Wind Picture Archives: 68, 69; Historical Pictures Service: 70; North Wind Picture Archives: 71, 72, 73, 74; Historical Pictures Service: 76; North Wind Picture Archives: 77; H. Armstrong Roberts: 78; Historical Pictures Service: 79, 81 (2 photos), 84, 85; North Wind Picture Archives: 87 (top); Sophia Smith Collection, Smith College, Northampton, Massachusetts: 87 (bottom); North Wind Picture Archives: 88 (top); U.S. Bureau of Printing and Engraving: 88 (bottom); Sophia Smith Collection, Smith College, Northampton, Massachusetts: 89; North Wind Picture Archives: 90 (bottom left and middle); Historical Pictures Service: 90 (top right and bottom right); AP/Wide World Photos: 90 (top left), 91; UPI/Bettmann Newsphotos: 92 (left); H. Armstrong Roberts: 92 (right); Standard Oil (NJ) Photographic Archive, University of Louisville: 92 (center); AP/Wide World Photos: 93; H. Armstrong Roberts: 94 (left); Historical Pictures Service: 94 (right), 95; U.S. Bureau of Printing and Engraving: 96 (9 photos); North Wind Picture Archives: 97, 98; Historical Pictures Service: 99; North Wind Picture Archives: 100; Historical Pictures Service: 102; Moorland-Spingarn Research Center, Howard University: 104; Historical Pictures Service: 106; AP/Wide World Photos: 107; Historical Pictures Service: 109; UPI/Bettmann Newsphotos: 111; AP/Wide World Photos: 113; Sophia Smith Collection, Smith College, Northampton, Massachusetts: 114; Historical Pictures Service: 116, 117 (top); UPI/Bettmann Newsphotos: 117 (bottom); AP/Wide World Photos: 119; UPI/Bettmann Newsphotos: 120; AP/Wide World Photos: 121, 123; Historical Pictures Service: 124 (right); UPI/Bettmann Newsphotos: 124 (left); AP/Wide World Photos: 125; Historical Pictures Service: 127; H. Armstrong Roberts: 129; Historical Pictures Service: 131; AP/Wide World Photos: 135; UPI/Bettmann Newsphotos: 137; Historical Pictures Service: 139; UPI/Bettmann Newsphotos: 141, 143 (left); H. Armstrong Roberts: 143 (right); UPI/Bettmann Newsphotos: 144; H. Armstrong Roberts: 146, 148 (left); UPI/Bettmann Newsphotos: 148 (right); Historical Pictures Service: 150; AP/Wide World Photos: 151, 153 (2 photos); UPI/Bettmann Newsphotos: 154, 155, 156, 157, 158; AP/Wide World: 160; UPI/Bettmann Newsphotos: 162, 163; AP/Wide World Photos: 164; UPI/Bettmann Newsphotos: 166 (bottom); Historical Pictures Service: 166 (top), 167 (bottom); AP/Wide World Photos: 167 (top); Historical Pictures Service: 168 (2 photos), 169 (bottom); UPI/Bettmann Newsphotos: 169 (top), 170 (top); AP/Wide World Photos: 170 (bottom); UPI/Bettmann Newsphotos: 171; Moorland-Spingarn Research Center, Howard University: 172; Historical Pictures Service: 173; Signal Corps Photo: 174 (left); U.S. Air Force Photos: 174 (right); UPI/Bettmann Newsphotos: 175 (top); AP/Wide World Photos: 175 (bottom); EKM-Nepenthe: 176; Historical Pictures Service: 177; UPI/Bettmann Newsphotos: 178; Courtesy American Civil Liberties Union: 179; Historical Pictures Service: 180; AP/Wide World Photos: 181; Historical Pictures Service: 182; U.S. Bureau of Printing and Engraving: 183 (9 photos); AP/Wide World Photos: 184; AP/Wide

World Photos: 188 (right); Ankers Capitol Photographers: 188 (left); H. Armstrong Roberts: 186; Historical Pictures Service: 190; AP/Wide World Photos: 191, 193 (2 photos), 196; UPI/Bettmann Newsphotos: 198; Historical Pictures Service: 199; UPI/Bettmann Newsphotos: 200; AP/Wide World Photos: 201, 203; UPI/Bettmann Newsphotos: 204; AP/Wide World Photos: 206, 207; UPI/Bettmann Newsphotos: 209; AP/Wide World Photos: 210, 211, 212, 213; AP/Wide World Photos: 215, 217, 218, 221, 222; UPI/Bettmann Newsphotos: 223; AP/Wide World Photos: 226, 227; UPI/Bettmann Newsphotos: 228, 230, 232; AP/Wide World Photos: 233; UPI/Bettmann Newsphotos: 236; H. Armstrong Roberts: 240; North Wind Picture Archives: 243; Photri: 244; UPI/Bettmann Newsphotos: 245; AP/Wide World Photos: 246, 247, 249, 251, 253 (2 photos); UPI/Bettmann Newsphotos: 254, 256; AP/Wide World Photos: 257, 259, 260, 261, 262, 263, 264; UPI/Bettmann Newsphotos: 267 (right); AP/Wide World Photos: 267 (left), 269 (2 photos), 270, 271; UPI/Bettmann Newsphotos: 272, 273; AP/Wide World Photos: 274; UPI/Bettmann Newsphotos: 275, 277; AP/Wide World Photos: 278, 279 (2 photos); UPI/Bettmann Newsphotos: 281, 283, 284, 286; AP/Wide World Photos: 287; The Bettmann Archive: 289; AP/Wide World Photos: 292, 294; UPI/Bettmann Newsphotos: 295, 297 (left); AP/Wide World Photos: 297 (right); UPI/Bettmann Newsphotos: 299, 300, 302; AP/Wide World Photos: 304, 307, 309; UPI/Bettmann Newsphotos: 310; AP/Wide World Photos: 312, 313, 314, 317; UPI/Bettmann Newsphotos: 318, 319, 320, 321, 322; AP/Wide World Photos: 333 (2 photos), 324 (2 photos); UPI/Bettmann Newsphotos: 325; AP/Wide World Photos: 326; UPI/Bettmann Newsphotos: 327; AP/Wide World Photos: 328 (2 photos), 329, 330 (2 photos), 331, 332; UPI/Bettmann Newsphotos: 333; AP/Wide World Photos: 334 (2 photos); U.S. Bureau of Printing and Engraving: 337 (6 photos); Official White House Photo—David Valdez: 337 (1 photo)

ABOUT THE AUTHORS

Patricia and Fredrick McKissack are freelance writers and editors who own All-Writing Services, a family business located in St. Louis, Missouri. They are well-known authors of children's books, which include the Start-Off stories produced by Childrens Press and the award-winning Christopher series. In 1985, the McKissacks won two C. S. Lewis Silver Awards for outstanding contribution in the area of children's literature for *It's the Truth, Christopher,* and *Abram, Abram, Where Are We Going.*

Several of Pat's biographies and picture books have received excellent reviews, especially *Flossie and the Fox*, which the Kirkus Book Review called a "perfect picture book."

In addition to writing, the McKissacks are often speakers at educational meetings, workshops, and seminars. Since 1975, Pat has taught writing for the University of Missouri Continuing Education program. Several of her students have gone on to become published authors.

The McKissacks are former Tennesseans who presently live in a large, remodeled city house in St. Louis. They are the parents of three sons.